EVIDENCE-BASED TREATMENT PLANNING FOR DEPRESSION

EVIDENCE-BASED TREATMENT PLANNING FOR DEPRESSION

DVD COMPANION WORKBOOK

ARTHUR E. JONGSMA, JR.

AND

TIMOTHY J. BRUCE

WILEY

John Wiley & Sons, Inc.

Contents

Introduction

This *Workbook* is a supplement to the *Evidence-Based Treatment Planning for Depression* DVD, which is focused on informing mental health therapists, addiction counselors, and students in these fields about empirically informed psychological treatment planning.

Organization

In this *Workbook* you will find in each chapter:

- ➤ Summary highlights of content shown in the DVD
- ➤ Chapter review discussion questions
- ➤ Chapter review test questions
- ➤ Chapter references

In appropriate chapters, the references are divided into those for Empirical Support, those for Clinical Resources, and those for Bibliotherapy Resources. The Empirical Support references are selected studies or reviews of the empirical work supporting the efficacy for the treatments discussed in the chapter. Clinical Resources are books, manuals, or other resources for clinicians that describe the application, or "how-to," of the treatments discussed. Bibliotherapy Resources are selected publications, on topics relevant to the DVD content, and that may be helpful to clients or laypersons.

Examples of client homework are included at www.wiley.com/go/depressionwb, designed to enhance understanding of therapeutic interventions, in addition to being potentially useful clinically. In Appendix A, correct and incorrect answers to all chapter review test questions are explained.

Chapter Points

This DVD is electronically marked with chapter points that delineate the beginning of discussion sections throughout the program. You may skip to any one of these chapter points in the video by clicking on the forward arrow. The chapter points for this program are as follows:

- DSM Criteria for Depression
- Six Steps to a Treatment Plan
- History of EST Movement
- Introduction to ESTs for Depression
- Integrating ESTs for Depression into Treatment Planning
- Cognitive Restructuring
- Behavioral Activation
- Personal and Interpersonal Skills Training and Problem-Solving
- Interpersonal Therapy
- Other Common Approaches to Treatment
- Relapse Prevention

Series Rationale

Evidence-based practice (EBP) is steadily becoming the standard of mental health-care, as it has in medical healthcare. Borrowing from the Institute of Medicine's definition (Institute of Medicine, 2001), the American Psychological Association (APA) has defined EBP as, "the integration of the best available research with clinical expertise in the context of patient characteristics, culture, and preferences" (American Psychological Association Presidential Task Force on Evidence-Based Practice [APA], 2006).

Professional organizations such as the American Psychological Association, National Association of Social Workers, and the American Psychiatric Association, as well as consumer organizations such the National Alliance for the Mentally Ill (NAMI), are endorsing EBP. At the federal level, a major joint initiative of the National Institute of Mental Health and Department of Health and Human Services' Substance Abuse and Mental Health Services Administration (SAMHSA) focuses on promoting, implementing, and evaluating evidence-based mental health programs and practices within state mental health systems (APA, 2006). In some practice settings, EBP is even becoming mandated. It is clear that the call for evidence-based practice is being increasingly sounded.

Unfortunately, many mental healthcare providers cannot or do not stay abreast of results from clinical research and how these results can inform their practices. Although it has rightfully been argued that the relevance of some research to the clinician's needs is weak, there are products of clinical research whose efficacy has been established and whose effectiveness in the community setting has received support. Clinicians and clinicians-in-training interested in empirically informing their treatments could benefit from educational programs that make this goal more easily attainable.

This series of DVDs and companion workbooks is designed to introduce clinicians and students to the process of empirically informing their psychotherapy treatment plans. The series begins with an introduction to the efforts to identify research-supported treatments and how the products of these efforts can be used to inform treatment planning. The other programs in the series focus on empirically informed treatment planning for each of several commonly seen clinical problems. In each problem-focused DVD, issues involved in defining or diagnosing the presenting problem are reviewed. Research-supported treatments for the problem are described, as well as the process used to identify them. Viewers are then systematically guided through the process of creating a treatment plan and shown how the plan can be informed by goals, objectives, and interventions consistent with those of the identified research-supported treatments. Example vignettes of selected interventions are also provided.

This series is intended to be educational and informative in nature and not meant to be a substitute for clinical training in the specific interventions discussed and demonstrated. References to empirical support of the treatments described, clinical resource material, and training opportunities are provided.

Presenters

Dr. Art Jongsma is the Series Editor and coauthor of the Practice*Planners*® series [1] published by John Wiley & Sons. He has authored or coauthored more than 40

Exhibit I.1   Dr. Tim Bruce and Dr. Art Jongsma

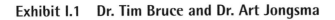

---

[1]These books are updated frequently, check with the publisher for the latest edition.

books in this series. Among the books included in this series are the highly regarded *The Complete Adult Psychotherapy Treatment Planner, The Adolescent* and *The Child Psychotherapy Treatment Planners,* and *The Addiction Treatment Planner.* All of these books, along with *The Severe and Persistent Mental Illness Treatment Planner, The Family Therapy Treatment Planner, The Veterans and Active Duty Military Psychotherapy Treatment Planner, The Couples Psychotherapy Treatment Planner,* and *The Older Adult Psychotherapy Treatment Planner* are informed with objectives and interventions that are supported by research evidence.

Dr. Jongsma also created the clinical record management software tool, Thera*Scribe,* which uses point-and-click technology to easily develop, store, and print treatment plans, progress notes, and homework assignments. He has conducted treatment planning and software training workshops for mental health professionals around the world.

Dr. Jongsma's clinical career began as a psychologist in a large private psychiatric hospital. He worked in the hospital for about 10 years and then transitioned to outpatient work in his own private practice clinic, Psychological Consultants, in Grand Rapids, Michigan for 25 years. He has been writing best-selling books and software for mental health professionals since 1995.

Dr. Timothy Bruce is a Professor and Associate Chair of the Department of Psychiatry and Behavioral Medicine at the University of Illinois, College of Medicine in Peoria, Illinois, where he also directs medical student education. He is a licensed clinical psychologist who completed his graduate training at SUNY–Albany, under the mentorship of Dr. David Barlow, and his residency training at Wilford Hall Medical Center, under the direction of Dr. Robert Klepac. In addition to maintaining an active clinical practice at the university, Dr. Bruce has authored numerous publications including books, professional journal articles, book chapters, and professional educational materials, many on the topic of evidence-based practice. Most recently, he has served as the contributing editor empirically informing Dr. Jongsma's best-selling Practice*Planners*® series.

Dr. Bruce is also Executive Director of the Center for the Dissemination of Evidence-based Mental Health Practices, a state- and federally funded initiative to disseminate evidence-based psychological and pharmacological practices across Illinois. Highly recognized as an educator, Dr. Bruce has received nearly two dozen awards for his teaching of students and professionals during his career.

References

American Psychological Association Presidential Task Force on Evidence-Based Practice. (2006). Evidence-based practice in psychology. *American Psychologist, 61*(4), 271–285.

Berghuis, D., Jongsma, A., & Bruce, T. (2006). *The severe and persistent mental illness treatment planner* (2nd ed). Hoboken, NJ: John Wiley & Sons.

Dattilio, F., Jongsma, A., & Davis, S. (2009). *The family therapy treatment planner* (2nd ed.). Hoboken, NJ: John Wiley & Sons.

Institute of Medicine. (2001). *Crossing the quality chasm: A new health system for the 21st century.* Washington, DC: National Academy Press.

Jongsma, A., Peterson, M., & Bruce, T. (2006). *The complete adult psychotherapy treatment planner* (4th ed.). Hoboken, NJ: John Wiley & Sons.

Jongsma, A., Peterson, M., McInnis, W. & Bruce, T. (2006a). *The adolescent psychotherapy treatment planner* (4th ed.). Hoboken, NJ: John Wiley & Sons.

Jongsma, A., Peterson, M., McInnis, W., & Bruce, T. (2006b). *The child psychotherapy treatment planner* (4th ed.). Hoboken, NJ: John Wiley & Sons.

Moore, B., & Jongsma, A. (2009). *The veterans and active duty military psychotherapy treatment planner.* Hoboken, NJ: John Wiley & Sons.

Perkinson, R., Jongsma, A., & Bruce, T. (2009). *The addiction treatment planner* (4th ed.). Hoboken, NJ: John Wiley & Sons.

1

What Are the DSM Criteria for Depression?

Diagnosing Mood Disorders Such as Major Depressive Disorder

Consistent with the Diagnostic and Statistical Manual of Mental Disorders (DSM-IV-TR; APA, 2000), the first step in diagnosing any mood disorder is to assess for any current or past *mood episodes*, which are clusters of specific mood symptoms that occur over a period of time.

The four types of mood episodes to consider are shown below:

MOOD EPISODES
1. Manic
2. Hypomanic
3. Major Depressive
4. Mixed

These episodes are then used to make the diagnosis of the appropriate *mood disorder*.

In the DSM, mood disorders may be *bipolar*, meaning that there has been or currently is evidence of a manic, hypomanic, or mixed episode in the clinical picture, or they may be *unipolar*, meaning that there is evidence of one or more *major depressive episodes* (MDEs) or dysthymia, without any current or past manic, hypomanic, or mixed episodes.

It is important to note that bipolar mood disorders may contain past or a present MDE in the clinical picture, in addition to the manic, hypomanic, or mixed episodes that define them. Unipolar mood disorders, however, cannot contain past or present manic, hypomanic, or mixed episodes. The presence of these types of episodes indicates a bipolar mood disorder.

MOOD DISORDERS
1. Bipolar
2. Unipolar

Bipolar I, bipolar II, and a chronic low-level mood disturbance called *cyclothymia* are the bipolar mood disorders, shown below:

BIPOLAR MOOD DISORDERS
- Bipolar Disorder I: A past or present manic or mixed episode. (May include a MDE)
- Bipolar Disorder II: A past or present hypomanic episode AND a past or present MDE, with no manic or mixed episodes. (Must include a MDE)
- Cyclothymia: Chronic low-level hypomanic and depressive symptoms.

Major Depressive Disorder and a chronic low-level version of depression called Dysthymia are the Unipolar Mood Disorders.

UNIPOLAR MOOD DISORDERS
- Major Depressive Disorder
- Dysthymia

Major Depressive Disorder

For an individual to be diagnosed with major depressive disorder, they must have experienced at least one MDE but no manic, hypomanic, or mixed episodes.

DIAGNOSTIC CRITERIA FOR MAJOR DEPRESSIVE DISORDER
- One or more MDEs
- No current or past manic, hypomanic, or mixed episodes

What constitutes an MDE

Key Point

An acronym useful for remembering the features of a depressive episode is SIGECAPSS, in which each letter of the word stands for a specific feature of the episode.

SIGECAPSS
Sadness
Interest
Guilt
Energy
Concentration
Appetite
Psychomotor
Sleep
Suicidality

An MDE is characterized by the presence of at least five SIGECAPSS, occurring for at least two weeks, and representing a change from previous functioning.

It is important to note that at least one of the features must be a depressed (or irritable) mood or a loss of interest or pleasure (the first S and the I in the SIGECAPSS acronym).

The SIGECAPSS
S—Sadness

- In depression, the mood is depressed most of the day, nearly every day. This may be indicated by either the report of the client (e.g., feels sad or empty) or observations made by others (e.g., appears tearful).
- Note that depression can also be characterized by an *irritable* mood, particularly in children.

I—Interest

- In depression, there is often markedly diminished interest or pleasure in all, or almost all, activities most of the day, nearly every day.

G—Guilt

➢ Feelings of worthlessness or excessive or inappropriate guilt may be present, and are not merely self-reproach or guilt about having the disorder.

E—Energy

➢ Depressed individuals often complain of excessive fatigue or loss of energy.

C—Concentration

➢ They often describe or show impairment in their ability to think, concentrate, or make decisions.

A—Appetite

➢ In its typical form, depression causes a diminished appetite and unintended weight loss. In atypical depression, appetite is increased or weight is gained.

P—Psychomotor

➢ In depression, psychomotor behavior (referring to the way one moves and gestures, including speech rate) may be either slowed or, conversely, show agitation.

S—Sleep

➢ As with appetite and weight, depression typically interferes with sleep, but may cause excessive sleep in its "atypical" expression.

S—Suicidality

➢ Of course, some individuals suffering depression may have thoughts of death and dying. They may have thoughts or have a plan for taking their own life, and in some cases may have attempted suicide.

DIAGNOSTIC CRITERIA FOR AN MDE
- Five (5) or more SIGECAPSS present during the same two-week period
- Symptoms represent a change from previous functioning
- At least one is depressed (or irritable) mood, or a loss of interest or pleasure.

In addition, the SIGECAPSS cannot occur along with manic symptoms, such as accelerated speech, flight of ideas, or heightened impulsivity, as seen in what is called a mixed episode. Mixed episodes are treated diagnostically like manic episodes, in that their presence represents a bipolar mood disturbance.

Finally, the depressive symptoms cause clinically significant distress or disability through impairment in social, occupational, or other important areas of functioning.

Chapter Review

1. Discuss the relationship between mood episodes and mood disorders.
2. What are the four major types of mood episodes?
3. What are the bipolar and unipolar mood disorders?
4. What is the acronym for remembering the criteria of an MDE?
5. For what does each letter of the acronym stand?
6. What are the diagnostic criteria for major depressive disorder?

Chapter Review Test Questions

1. Which of the following meets the criteria for an MDE, assuming its presence for more than two weeks?

   A. Fatigue, insomnia, withdrawal, loss of appetite, concern about symptoms
   B. Irritability, agitation, argumentativeness, disorganized thinking, impulsivity
   C. Sadness, fatigue, excessive appetite, excessive sleeping, psychomotor slowing
   D. Sadness, anxiety, recent loss of job, insomnia, worry

2. A person currently meeting the criteria for an MDE could have which of the following types of mood disorders?

   A. Unipolar
   B. Bipolar
   C. Either unipolar or bipolar
   D. Neither unipolar nor bipolar

Chapter Reference

American Psychiatric Association. (2000). *Diagnostic and statistical manual of mental disorders* (4th ed., text revised). Washington, DC: American Psychiatric Association.

What Are the Six Steps in Building a Treatment Plan?

Step 1: **Identify primary and secondary problems**
> ➤ Use evidence-based psychosocial assessment procedures to determine the most significant problem, making sure to include client input as to pain and disruption in functioning.

Step 2: **Describe the problem's behavioral manifestations (symptom pattern)**
> ➤ Note how the problem symptoms reveal themselves in your unique client.

Step 3: **Make a diagnosis based on DSM/ICD criteria**
> ➤ Compare the client's symptoms to the criteria for a diagnostic label from DSM or ICD.

Step 4: **Specify long-term goals**
> ➤ These are broad statements describing the anticipated end result of treatment.

Step 5: **Create short-term objectives**
> ➤ Objectives for the client to achieve should be stated in measurable or observable terms so accountability is enhanced.

Step 6: **Select therapeutic interventions**
> ➤ At least one interventional action to be implemented by the therapist should be paired with each client objective to assist the client in reaching that specific objective.

Key Point

One important aspect of effective treatment planning is that each plan should be tailored to the individual client's unique problems and needs. Treatment plans should not be boilerplate, even if clients have similar problems. Consistent with the definition of an evidence-based practice in psychology advanced by the American Psychological Association Presidential Task Force on Evidence-Based Practice (APA, 2006), the individual's strengths and weaknesses, unique stressors, cultural and social network family circumstances, and symptom patterns must be considered in developing a treatment strategy. Clinicians should rely on their own good clinical judgment and select interventions that are appropriate for the distinctive individual with whom they are working.

Chapter Review

1. What are the six steps involved in developing a psychotherapy treatment plan?

Chapter Review Test Questions

1. A psychotherapy treatment plan can be drawn up without a diagnosis. For example, a good case formulation can be the basis of therapy. Why is it important to consider the diagnosis when developing a plan that could be informed by empirically supported treatments (ESTs)?

   A. A diagnosis is necessary to judge response to the EST.
   B. It is not necessary to consider diagnosis in empirically informed treatment planning.
   C. Some ESTs were developed and studied using diagnosis as inclusion criteria.
   D. Treatment may require medication, which typically requires diagnosis to be specified.

2. The statement "Identify, challenge, and change biased self-talk supportive of depression" is an example of which of the following steps in a treatment plan?

   A. A primary problem
   B. A short-term objective
   C. A symptom manifestation
   D. A treatment intervention

Chapter References

American Psychological Association Presidential Task Force on Evidence-Based Practice. (2006). Evidence-based practice in psychology. *American Psychologist*, *61(4)*, 271–285.

Jongsma, A. (2005). Psychotherapy treatment plan writing. In G.P. Koocher, J.C. Norcross, & S.S. Hill (Eds.), *Psychologists' desk reference* (2nd ed., pp. 232–236). New York: Oxford University Press.

Jongsma, A., Peterson, M., & Bruce, T. (2005). *The complete adult psychotherapy treatment planner* (4th ed.). Hoboken, NJ: John Wiley & Sons.

CHAPTER 3

What Is the Brief History of the Empirically Supported Treatments Movement?

In the United States, the effort to identify empirically supported treatments (ESTs) began with an initiative of the American Psychological Association's Division 12— The Society of Clinical Psychology.

In 1993, APA's Division 12 President David Barlow initiated a task group, chaired by Diane Chambless, charged with the review of psychotherapy outcome literature to identify psychological treatments whose efficacy had been demonstrated through clinical research.

This group was originally called the Task Force on the Promotion and Dissemination of Psychological Procedures, and became the Task Force on Psychological Interventions.

Note: On the DVD, our reference to the Task Force on Psychological Interventions refers to the work of both task groups.

Process Used to Identify ESTs

Reviewers first established two primary sets of criteria for judging the evidence base supporting any particular therapy. One was labeled *well-established*, the other *probably efficacious* (Figure 3.1).

CRITERIA FOR EVALUATING EFFICACY OF PSYCHOLOGICAL TREATMENTS
- Well-Established
- Probably Efficacious

Figure 3.1

Specific Criteria for Well-Established and Probably Efficacious Treatments

Criteria for Well-Established Treatments

For a psychological treatment to be considered *well-established*, the evidence base supporting it had to be characterized by the following:

I. At least two good between group design experiments demonstrating efficacy in one or more of the following ways:

   A. Superior (statistically significantly so) to pill or psychological placebo or to another treatment

   B. Equivalent to an already established treatment in experiments with adequate sample sizes

OR

II. A large series of single case design experiments (n > 9) demonstrating efficacy; these experiments must:

   A. Use good experimental designs

   B. Compare the intervention to another treatment, as in IA

Further Criteria for Both I And II

III. Experiments must be conducted with treatment manuals.

IV. Characteristics of the client samples must be clearly specified.

V. Effects must have been demonstrated by at least two different investigators or investigating teams.

Criteria for Probably Efficacious Treatments

For a psychological treatment to be considered *probably efficacious*, the evidence base supporting it had to meet the following criteria:

I. Two experiments showing the treatment is superior (statistically significantly so) to a waiting-list control group

OR

II. One or more experiments meeting the well-established treatment criteria IA or IB, III, and IV, but not V

OR

III. A small series of single case design experiments (n > 3) otherwise meeting well-established treatment criteria

---

Adapted from: Chambless, D. L., Baker, M. J., Baucom, D. H., Beutler, L. E., Calhoun, K. S., Crits-Christoph, P., Daiuto, A., DeRubeis, R., Detweiler, J., Haaga, D. A. F., Bennett Johnson, S., McCurry, S., Mueser, K. T., Pope, K. S., Sanderson, W. C., Shoham, V., Stickle, T., Williams, D. A., & Woody, S. R. (1998). Update on empirically validated therapies, II. *The Clinical Psychologist, 51(1)*, 3–16.

Products of EST Reviews

The products of these reviews can be found in the Division 12 groups' final two reports.

> ➤ In the first, 47 ESTs are identified (Chambless et al., 1996).
> ➤ In the final, the list had grown to 71 ESTs (Chambless et al., 1998).
> ➤ In 1999, The Society of Clinical Psychology, Division 12, took full ownership of maintaining the growing list. The current list and information center can be found on its Web site at: www.psychologicaltreatments.org.

Around this same time, other groups emerged, using the same or similar criteria, to review literature related to other populations, problems, and interventions. Examples include the following:

> ➤ Children (Lonigan & Elbert, 1998)
> ➤ Pediatric Psychology (Spirito, 1999)
> ➤ Older Adults (Gatz, 1998)
> ➤ Adult, Child, Marital, Family Therapy (Kendall & Chambless, 1998).
> ➤ Psychopharmacology and Psychological Treatments (Nathan & Gorman, 1998; 2002; 2007)
> ➤ For those interested in comparing and contrasting the criteria used by various review groups, see Chambless and Ollendick (2001).

Other Organizational Reviewers of Evidence–Based Psychological Treatments

> ➤ Great Britain was at the forefront of the effort to identify evidence-based treatments and develop guidelines for practice. The latest products of their work can be found at the Web site for the National Institute for Health and Clinical Excellence (NICE): www.nice.org.uk.
> ➤ The Substance Abuse and Mental Health Service Administration (SAMHSA) has also begun an initiative to evaluate, identify, and provide information on various mental health practices. Their work, entitled "The National Registry of Evidence-based Programs and Practices," can be found online at www.nrepp .samhsa.gov.

── **Key Point** ──

The Web site www.therapyadvisor.com provides descriptions, references to empirical support, clinical training materials, and training opportunities for many of the empirically supported treatments identified by the original Division 12 review groups.

Chapter Review

1. How did Division 12 of the APA identify ESTs?
2. What are the primary differences between *well-established* and *probably efficacious* criteria used to identify ESTs?
3. Where can information about ESTs and evidence-based practices be found?

Chapter Review Test Questions

1. What statement best describes the process used to identify ESTs?

    A. Consumers of mental health services nominated therapies.
    B. Experts came to a consensus based on their experiences with the treatments.
    C. Researchers submitted their works.
    D. Task groups reviewed the literature using selection criteria.

2. Based on the differences in their criteria, in which of the following ways are *well-established* treatments different than those classified as *probably efficacious?*

    A. Only probably efficacious treatments allowed the use of single case design experiments.
    B. Only well-established treatments allowed studies comparing the treatment to a psychological placebo.
    C. Only well-established treatments required demonstration by at least two different, independent investigators or investigating teams.
    D. Only well-established treatments allowed studies comparing the treatment to a pill placebo.

Chapter References

Chambless, D. L., & Ollendick, T. H. (2001). Empirically supported psychological interventions: Controversies and evidence. *Annual Review of Psychology, 52,* 685–716.

Chambless, D. L., Sanderson, W. C., Shoham, V., Bennett Johnson, S., Pope, K. S., Crits-Christoph, P., Baker, M., Johnson, B., Woody, S. R., Sue, S., Beutler, L., Williams, D. A., & McCurry, S. (1996). An update on empirically validated therapies. *The Clinical Psychologist, 49,* 5–18.

Chambless, D. L., Baker, M. J., Baucom, D. H., Beutler, L. E., Calhoun, K. S., Crits-Christoph, P., Daiuto, A., DeRubeis, R., Detweiler, J., Haaga, D. A. F., Bennett Johnson, S., McCurry, S., Mueser, K. T., Pope, K. S., Sanderson, W. C., Shoham, V., Stickle, T., Williams, D. A., & Woody, S. R. (1998). Update on empirically validated therapies, II. *The Clinical Psychologist, 51(1),* 3–16.

Gatz, M., Fiske, A., Fox, L. S., Kaskie, B., Kasl-Godley, J. E., et al. (1998). Empirically validated psychological treatments for older adults. *Journal of Mental Health and Aging, 41,* 9–46.

Kendall, P. C., & Chambless, D. L. (Eds.). (1998). Empirically supported psychological therapies [Special issue]. *Journal of Consulting and Clinical Psychology, 66 (3)* 151–162.

Lonigan, C. J., & Elbert, J. C. (Eds.). (1998). Special Issue on Empirically Supported Psychosocial Interventions for Children. *Journal of Clinical Child Psychology, 27,* 138–226.

Nathan, P. E., & Gorman, J. M. (Eds.). (1998). *A Guide to Treatments That Work.* New York: Oxford University Press.

Nathan, P. E., & Gorman, J. M. (Eds.). (2002). *A Guide to Treatments That Work, Second Edition.* New York: Oxford University Press.

Nathan, P. E., & Gorman, J. M. (Eds.). (2007). *A Guide to Treatments That Work, Third Edition.* New York: Oxford University Press.

Spirito, A. (Ed.). (1999). Empirically supported treatments in pediatric psychology [Special issue]. *Journal of Pediatric Psychology, 24,* 87–174.

4

What Are the Identified Empirically Supported Treatments for Depression?

Empirically informing a treatment plan involves integrating aspects of identified empirically supported treatments (ESTs) into each step of the treatment planning process discussed previously. The psychotherapy outcome literature on depression is one of the most researched in the field. Consequently, several therapies have been identified as empirically supported.

The APA's Division 12 (The Society of Clinical Psychology) has identified six therapies with strong research support, meaning that they have met the original Division 12 criteria for a well-established EST.

Key Points

WELL-ESTABLISHED ESTs FOR DEPRESSION
- Behavioral Therapy/Behavioral Activation
- Cognitive Therapy/Cognitive Restructuring
- Interpersonal Therapy
- Problem-Solving Therapy
- Self-Management/Self-Control Therapy
- Cognitive Behavioral Analysis System of Psychotherapy

In addition, there have been a number of therapies meeting the original Division 12 criteria for probably efficacious. These are:

- Acceptance and commitment therapy
- Behavioral couples therapy
- Emotion-focused therapy
- Short-term psychodynamic therapy

Well-Established ESTs for Depression

Behavioral Therapy/Behavioral Activation

Behavioral therapies for depression focus on problematic relationships between behavior and the environment in which it occurs.

From the perspective of this model, depression is associated with low positive reinforcement and high aversive consequences in the environment.

Those struggling with depression tend to disengage from their environment through withdrawal or avoidance. This is thought to perpetuate depression by reducing exposure to potentially rewarding and positively reinforcing experiences that could help lift the depression.

Behavioral therapies commonly use techniques such as skills training and activity scheduling to increase engagement in potentially rewarding experiences through which the client derives pleasure, a sense of mastery, purpose, and other positively reinforcing and otherwise anti-depressant emotions.

BEHAVIORAL THERAPIES FOCUS ON:
- Skills training
- Increasing rewarding activities
- Decreasing aversive consequences
- Increasing experiences of pleasure, mastery, and purpose

Cognitive Therapy

Cognitive therapy (CT) for depression evolved from Beck's cognitive theory. From the perspective of this model, depression is maintained by biased information processing and maladaptive beliefs.

In CT, clients learn to identify, challenge, and change biased thoughts to alternatives that correct for the biases, through the clinician's use of the *cognitive restructuring technique*. In *prediction testing*, the biased and alternative thoughts are converted into predictions and tested against reality in what is termed a *behavioral experiment*. Later therapy may explore underlying assumptions and beliefs reflected in biased self-talk that put the client at risk for relapse or recurrence.

COGNITIVE THERAPY (CT) FOCUSES ON:
- Biased self-talk
- Alternative self-talk
- Prediction testing
- Behavioral experiments

Cognitive therapists use a variety of cognitive restructuring strategies and techniques to help depressed clients address their thinking, as shown below.

CT STRATEGIES AND TECHNIQUES
- Psychoeducation
- Guided discovery
- Socratic questioning
- Role playing
- Imagery
- Behavioral experiments

Cognitive therapy includes many techniques that derive from behavioral traditions, including increasing activities and learning adaptive coping and problem-solving skills, as shown below:

OTHER TECHNIQUES USED IN CT
- Increasing activities
- Self-monitoring of mastery and pleasure
- Graded task assignments
- Coping and problem-solving skills

Interpersonal Therapy

The late Dr. Gerald Klerman and Dr. Myrna Weissman developed Interpersonal Therapy (IPT) for depression.

As Dr. Weissman notes, "IPT makes no assumption about the 'cause of depression,' but is based on the observation that depression occurs in an interpersonal context. By understanding and solving the current interpersonal problem(s) . . . associated with the onset of symptoms, the patient will both improve their life situation and relieve their symptoms."

The initial sessions of IPT are devoted to taking a detailed *interpersonal inventory* and formulating the patient's depression in interpersonal terms that can be related to some type of grief, a personal transition, disputes, or a lack of skills.

INTERPERSONAL THERAPY (IPT) FOCUSES ON:
- Assessing the client's *interpersonal inventory* of important past and present relationships
- Case formulation linking depression to grief, interpersonal role disputes, role transitions, and/or interpersonal deficits

Common therapeutic techniques used in IPT are those found in most psycho-therapies, as shown below:

IPT Strategies and Techniques
- Clarification
- Supportive listening
- Encouragement of affect
- Role playing
- Communication analysis

While IPT has been manualized, it is less directive than cognitive and behavioral therapies and does not use therapeutic "homework" in the way that BT or CT does.

Problem–Solving Therapy

Problem-solving therapy, or PST, teaches patients to more effectively approach and resolve problems in their lives. Through PST, clients learn to understand and change the nature of their problems, their reactions to them, or both, using a positive problem orientation and problem-solving skills.

Problem–Solving Therapy (PST)
- Positive Problem Orientation
- Problem-Solving Skills

Positive problem orientation refers to a motivational technique that helps clients understand that it is *normal* to have problems and that they can resolve them effectively by facing and solving them.

In PST, clients learn the steps for effective problem-solving and how to use these steps with current problems in living.

Problem–Solving Steps
- Define the problem specifically.
- Generate options for addressing the problem without evaluating them.
- Evaluate the generated options.
- Select the best solution and implement it.
- Evaluate the effectiveness of the plan.
- Keep, revise, or change plans based on the evaluation of its effectiveness.

Self-Management/Self-Control Therapy

Self-management/self-control therapy is a highly structured, manualized, cognitive-behavioral group therapy program for the treatment of depression. The program is typically presented in weekly sessions that are structured and involve homework.

This model characterizes depression as involving selective attention to negative events and immediate consequences of events; unreasonably stringent self-evaluative standards; negative, inaccurate attributions of responsibility for events; insufficient self-reinforcement; and excessive self-punishment.

Self-management therapy targets specific components of depression and teaches participants self-change techniques for modifying each target behavior. Its goals are to help clients accurately view their world, have a realistic sense of their abilities, set reasonable standards and goals, and control their behavior with feedback to themselves. Although often delivered in group format, the therapy can be delivered in individual format. It has been applied to the treatment of depression in children and adolescents, adults, and geriatric populations.

SELF-MANAGEMENT/SELF-CONTROL THERAPY FOCUSES ON:
- Helping clients accurately view their world
- Having a realistic sense of their abilities
- Setting reasonable standards and goals
- Controlling their behavior with feedback to themselves

Cognitive Behavioral Analysis System of Psychotherapy

The Cognitive Behavioral Analysis System of Psychotherapy (CBASP) is an integrative therapy for chronically depressed adults that combines components of cognitive, behavioral, interpersonal, and psychodynamic therapies.

According to this model, those with chronic depression are disconnected from their environment and do not get the feedback they need to help them adapt effectively.

The therapeutic relationship is actively used to help patients generate empathic behavior, identify and change interpersonal patterns related to depression, and heal interpersonal trauma.

CBASP CONSISTS OF THREE PRIMARY TECHNIQUES:
1. *Situational analysis*, a problem-solving technique designed to help the patient realize the consequences of his/her behavior on others and modify it
2. *Interpersonal discrimination exercises*, which help the patient examine past traumatic experiences with others and differentiate those from healthier relationships
3. *Behavioral skill training/rehearsal*, such as assertiveness training, which further helps depressed individuals modify maladaptive behavior

---

CBASP Focuses on:

- Helping the client realize the consequences of his/her behavior on others
- Examining past traumatic experiences
- Differentiating past traumatic relationships from healthier ones
- Developing adaptive skills

Chapter Review

1. Name the six ESTs for depression identified as *well-established* by Division 12 of the APA.

Chapter Review Test Questions

1. The therapeutic intervention that involves scheduling client activities that increase the client's exposure to rewarding feelings, such as pleasure, feeling worthwhile, feeling productive, and the like, is called:

   A. Behavioral activation
   B. Behavioral experiment
   C. Behavioral exposure
   D. Behavioral therapy

2. The practice of thoroughly assessing important past and present relationships with others is a prominent feature of which EST for depression?

   A. Behavior therapy
   B. Cognitive therapy
   C. Interpersonal therapy
   D. Problem-solving therapy

Selected Chapter References

Empirical Support for Behavior Therapy/Behavioral Activation

Areán, P. A., Gum. A., McCulloch, C. E., Bostrom, A., Gallagher-Thompson, D., & Thompson, L. (2005). Treatment of depression in low-income older adults. *Psychology and Aging, 20,* 601–609.

Cuipers, P. (1998). A psychoeducational approach to the treatment of depression: A meta-analysis of Lewinsohn's "Coping with Depression" course. *Behavior Therapy, 29,* 521–533.

Cuipers, P., van Straten, A., & Warmerdam, L. (2007). Behavioral activation treatments of depression: A meta-analysis. *Clinical Psychology Review, 27,* 318–326.

Dimidjian, S., Hollon, S. D., Dobson, K. S., Schmaling, K. B., Kohlenberg, R. J., Addis, M. E., et al. (2006). Randomized trial of behavioral activation, cognitive therapy, and antidepressant medication in the acute treatment of adults with major depression. *Journal of Consulting and Clinical Psychology, 74,* 638–670.

Gortner, E. T., Gollan, J. K., Dobson, K. S., & Jacobson, N. S. (1998). Cognitive-behavioral treatment for depression: Relapse prevention. *Journal of Consulting and Clinical Psychology, 66,* 377–384.

Jacobson, N. S., Dobson, K. S., Traux, P.A., Addis, M.E., Koerner, K., Gollan, E., et al. (1996). A component analysis of cognitive-behavioral treatment for depression. *Journal of Consulting and Clinical Psychology, 64,* 293–304.

Kuehner, C. (2005). An evaluation of the "Coping with Depression Course" for relapse prevention with unipolar depressed patients. *Psychotherapy and Psychosomatics, 74,* 254–259.

Miranda, J., Bernal, G., Lau, A., Kohn, L., Hwang, W., & LaFramboise, T. (2005). State of the science on psychosocial interventions for ethnic minorities. *Annual Review of Clinical Psychology, 1,* 113–142.

Clinical Resources

Jacobson, N. S., Martell, C. R. & Dimidjian, S. (2001). Behavioral activation treatment for depression: Returning to contextual roots. *Clinical Psychology: Science & Practice, 8,* 225-270.

Lewinsohn, P. M., Munoz, R., Youngren, M., & Zeiss, A. M. (1986). *Control Your Depression.* NY: Fireside.

Martell, C. R., Addis, M. E., & Jacobson, N. S. (2001). *Depression in context: Strategies for guided action.* New York: Norton.

Empirical Support for Cognitive/Cognitive–Behavioral Therapies

DeRubeis, R. J., Gelfand, L. A., Tang, T. Z., & Simons, A. (1999). Medications versus cognitive behavioral therapy for severely depressed outpatients: Meta-analysis of four randomized comparisons. *American Journal of Psychiatry, 156,* 1007–1013.

DeRubeis, R. J., Hollon, S. D., Amsterdam, J. D., Shelton, R. C., Young, P. R., Saloman, R. M., et al. (2005). Cognitive therapy vs. medications in the treatment of moderate to severe depression. *Archives of General Psychiatry, 62,* 409–416.

Elkin, I., Shea, M. T., Watkins, J. T., Imber, S. D., Sotsky, S. M., Collins, J. F., et al. (1989). National Institute of Mental Health Treatment of Depression Collaborative Research Program: General effectiveness of treatments. *Archives of General Psychiatry, 46,* 971–982.

Gloagen, V., Cottraux, J., Cucherat, M., & Blackburn, I. (1998). A meta-analysis of the effects of cognitive therapy in depressed patients. *Journal of Affective Disorders, 49,* 59–72.

Hollon, S. D., DeRubeis, R. J., Shelton, R. C., Amsterdam, J. D., Saloman, R. M., O'Reardon, J. P., et al. (2005). Prevention of relapse following cognitive therapy vs. medications in moderate to severe depression. *Archives of General Psychiatry, 62,* 417–422.

Hollon, S. D., Thase, M. E., & Markowitz, J. C. (2002). Treatment and prevention of depression. *Psychological Science in the Public Interest, 3,* 39–77.

Miranda, J., Bernal, G., Lau, A., Kohn, L., Hwang, W., & LaFramboise, T. (2005). State of the science on psychosocial interventions for ethnic minorities. *Annual Review of Clinical Psychology, 1,* 113–142.

Vittengl, J. R., Clark, L. A., Dunn, T. W., & Jarrett, R. B. (2007). Reducing relapse and recurrence in unipolar depression: A comparative meta-analysis of cognitive-behavioral therapy's effects. *Journal of Consulting and Clinical Psychology, 75,* 475–488.

Clinical Resources

Beck, J. S. (1995). *Cognitive therapy: Basics and beyond.* New York: Guilford.

Beck, A. T., Rush, A. J., Shaw, B. F., & Emery, G. (1979). *Cognitive therapy of depression.* New York: Guilford.

Empirical Support for Problem-Solving Therapy

Cuipers, P., van Straten, A., & Warmerdam, L. (2007). Problem-solving therapies for depression: A meta-analysis. *European Psychiatry, 22,* 9–15.

Gellis, Z. D., & Kenaley, B. (2007). Problem-solving therapy for depression in adults: A systematic review. *Research on Social Work Practice, 18,* 117–131.

Malouff, J. M., Thorsteinsson, E. B., Schutte, N. S. (2007). The efficacy of problem-solving therapy in reducing mental and physical health problems: A meta-analysis. *Clinical Psychology Review, 27,* 46–57.

Mynors-Wallis, L. M., Gath, D. H., Lloyd-Thomas, A. R., & Tomlinson, D. (1995). Randomised controlled trial comparing problem-solving treatment with amitriptyline and placebo for major depression in primary care. *British Medical Journal, 310,* 441–445.

Nezu, A. M. (1986). Efficacy of a social problem-solving approach for unipolar depression. *Journal of Consulting and Clinical Psychology, 54,* 196–202.

Nezu, A. M. (2004). Problem-solving and behavior therapy revisited. *Behavior Therapy, 35,* 1–33.

Clinical Resources

D'Zurilla, T. J., & Nezu, A. M. (2001). Problem-solving therapies. In K. Dobson (Ed.), *Handbook of cognitive-behavioral therapies* (2nd ed., pp. 211–245). NY: Guilford.

D'Zurilla, T. J., & Nezu, A. M. (2007). *Problem-solving therapy: A positive approach to clinical interventions* (3rd ed.). New York: Springer Publishing Co.

Nezu, A. M., Nezu C.M., & Perri, M.G. (1989). *Problem-solving therapy for depression: Theory, research, and clinical guidelines.* New York: John Wiley & Sons.

Empirical Support for Interpersonal Therapy

Bolton, P., Bass, J., Neugebauer, R., Clougherty, K. F., Verdeli, H., Wickramaratne, P. J., et al. (2003). Group interpersonal psychotherapy for depression in rural Uganda: A randomized controlled trial. *Journal of the American Medical Association, 289(23),* 3117–3124.

Cutler, J. L., Goldyne, A., Markowitz, J. C., Devlin, M. J., & Glick, R. A. (2004). Comparing cognitive behavioral therapy, interpersonal psychotherapy, and psychodynamic psychotherapy. *American Journal of Psychiatry, 161,* 1567–1573.

Elkin, I., Shea, M. T., Watkins, J. T., Imber, S. D., Sotsky, S. M., Collins, J. F., et al. (1989). National Institute of Mental Health Treatment of Depression Collaborative Research Program: General effectiveness of treatments. *Archives of General Psychiatry, 46,* 971–982.

Frank, E., Kupfer, D. J., Perel, J. M., Cornes, C., Jarrett, D. B., Mallinger, A. D., et al. (1990). Three-year outcomes for maintenance therapies in recurrent depression. *Archives of General Psychiatry, 47,* 1093–1099.

Frank, E., Kupfer, D. J., Wagner, E. F., McEachran, A., & Cornes, C. (1991). Efficacy of interpersonal psychotherapy as a maintenance treatment for recurrent depression: Contributing factors. *Archives of General Psychiatry, 48,* 1053–1059.

Hollon, S. D., Thase, M. E., & Markowitz, J. C. (2002). Treatment and prevention of depression. *Psychological Science in the Public Interest, 3,* 39–77. [Review article]

Klerman, G.L., DiMascio, A., Weissman, M.M., Prushoff, B.A., & Paykel, E.S. (1974). Treatment of depression by drugs and psychotherapy. *American Journal of Psychiatry, 131,* 186–191.

Kupfer, D. J., Frank, E., Perel, J. M., Cornes, C., Mallinger, A. G., Thase, M. E., et al. (1992). Five-year outcome for maintenance therapies in recurrent depression. *Archives of General Psychiatry, 49,* 769–773.

Shea, M. T., Elkin, S. D., Imber, S. D., Sotsky, J. T., Watkins, J. F., Collins, P. A., et al. (1992). Course of depressive symptoms over follow-up: Findings from the National Institute of Mental Health Treatment of Depression Collaborative Research Program. *Archives of General Psychiatry, 49,* 782–787.

Clinical Resources

Markowitz, J. C. (2003). Interpersonal psychotherapy for chronic depression. *Journal of Clinical Psychology: In Session, 59,* 847–858.

Weissman, M. M., Markowitz, J. C., & Klerman, G. L. (2000). *Comprehensive guide to interpersonal psychotherapy.* New York: Basic Books.

Wilfley, D. E., Mackenzie K. R., Welch R. R., Ayres V. E., & Weissman M. M. (2000). *Interpersonal psychotherapy for group.* New York: Basic Books.

Empirical Support for Self-Management/Self-Control Therapy

Dunn, N. J., Rehm, L. P., Schillaci, J., Souchek, J., Mehta, P., Ashton, C. M., et al. (2007). A randomized trial of self-management and psychoeducational group therapies for comorbid chronic posttraumatic stress disorder and depressive disorder. *Journal of Traumatic Stress, 20,* 221–237.

Fuchs, C. Z., & Rehm, L. P. (1977). A self-control behavior therapy program for depression. *Journal of Consulting and Clinical Psychology, 45,* 206–215.

Rehm, L. P. (1977). A self-control model of depression. *Behavior Therapy, 8,* 787–804.

Rehm, L. P., Fuchs, C. Z., Roth, D. M., Kornblith, S. J., & Romano, J. (1979). A comparison of self control and social skills treatments of depression. *Behavior Therapy, 10,* 429–442.

Reynolds, W. M., & Coats, K. I. (1986). A comparison of cognitive-behavioral therapy and relaxation training for the treatment of depression in adolescents. *Journal of Consulting and Clinical Psychology, 54,* 653–660.

Robinson-Whelen, S., Hughes, R. B., Taylor, H. B., Hall, J. W., & Rehm, L. P. (2007). Depression self-management program for rural women with physical disabilities. *Rehabilitation Psychology, 52,* 254–262.

Rokke, P. D., Tomhave, J. A., & Jocic, Z. (2000). Self-management therapy and educational group therapy for depressed elders. *Cognitive Therapy and Research, 24,* 99–119.

Roth, D., Bielski, R., Jones, M., Parker, W., & Osburn, G. (1982). A comparison of self-control therapy and combined self-control therapy and antidepressant medication in the treatment of depression. *Behavior Therapy, 13,* 133–144.

Thomas, J. R., Petry, T., & Goldman, J. (1987). Comparison of cognitive and behavioral self-control treatments of depression. *Psychological Reports, 60,* 975–982.

Van den Hout, J. H., Arntz, A., & Kunkels, F. H. (1995). Efficacy of a self-control therapy program in a psychiatric day-treatment center. *Acta Psychiatrika Scandinavia, 92(1),* 25–29.

Clinical Resources

Rehm, L. P. (2003). *Self-management therapy for depression*. Personal Improvement Computer Systems (PICS), Inc. **Retrieved August 27, 2009 from the NIMH project at www.therapyadvisor.com.**

Rehm, L. P. (1984). Self-management therapy for depression. *Advances in Behaviour Therapy and Research, 6,* 83–98.

Empirical Support for Cognitive Behavioral Analysis System of Psychotherapy

Keller, M. B., McCullough, J. P., Klein, D. N., Arnow, B., Dunner, D. L., Gelenberg, A. L., et al. (2000). A comparison of nefazodone, the cognitive behavioral analysis system of psychotherapy, and their combination for the treatment of chronic depression. *New England Journal of Medicine, 342,* 1462–1470.

Klein, D. N., Santiago, N. J., Vivian, D., Arnow, B. A., Blalock, J. A., Dunner, D. L., et al. (2004). Cognitive Behavioral Analysis System of Psychotherapy as a maintenance treatment for chronic depression. *Journal of Consulting and Clinical Psychology, 72,* 681–688.

Manber, R., Arnow, B.A., Blasey, C., Vivian, D., McCullough, J.P., Blalock, J.A., et al. (2003). Patient's therapeutic skill acquisition and response to psychotherapy, alone and in combination with medication. *Journal of Psychological Medicine, 33,* 693–702.

Nemeroff, C.B., Heim, C.M., Thase, M.E., Klein, D.N., Rush, A.J., Schatzberg, A.F., et al. (2003). Differential responses to psychotherapy versus pharmacotherapy in the treatment of patients with chronic forms of major depression and childhood trauma. *Proceedings of the National Academy of Sciences, 100,* 14293–14296.

Schatzberg, A. F., Rush, A. J., Arnow, B. A., Banks, P. L. C., Blalock, J. A., Borian, F. A., et al. (2005). Chronic depression: Medication (nefazodone) or psychotherapy (CBASP) is effective when the other is not. *Archives of General Psychiatry, 62,* 513–520.

Clinical Resources

McCullough, J. P. (2006). *Treating chronic depression with disciplined personal involvement: CBASP*. New York: Springer-Verlag.

McCullough, J. P. (2001). *Skills training manual for diagnosing and treating chronic depression: Cognitive behavioral analysis system of psychotherapy*. New York: Guilford.

McCullough, J. P. (2000). *Treatment for chronic depression: Cognitive behavioral analysis system of psychotherapy (CBASP)*. New York: Guilford Press.

Bibliotherapy Resources

Addis, M. E., & Martell, C. R. (2004). *Overcoming depression one step at a time: The new behavioral activation approach to getting your life back.* Oakland, CA: New Harbinger.

Bieling, P. J., Antony, M. M., & Beck, A. T. (2003). *Ending the depression cycle: A step-by-step guide for preventing relapse.* Oakland, CA: New Harbinger.

Burns, D. D. (1999). *Feeling good: The new mood therapy.* New York: HarperCollins.

Gilson, M., & Freemen, A. (2000). *Overcoming depression: A cognitive therapy approach for taming the depression beast: Client workbook.* New York: Oxford University Press.

Greenberger, D., & Padesky, C. (1995). *Mind over mood: Change how you feel by changing the way you think.* New York: Guilford Press.

Lewinsohn, P. (1992). *Control your depression.* New York: Fireside.

Martell, C. R., Addis, M. E., & Jacobson, N. S. (2001). *Depression in context: Strategies for guided action.* New York: Norton.

McCullough Jr., J. P. (2003). *Patient's manual for CBASP.* New York: Guilford Press.

Nezu, A. M. Nezu, C. M., & D'Zurilla, T. J. (2007). *Solving life's problems: A 5-step guide to enhanced well-being.* New York: Springer Publishing Co.

Pettit, J. W., Joiner, T. E., & Rehm, L. P. (2005). *The interpersonal solution to depression: A workbook for changing how you feel by changing how you relate.* Oakland, CA: New Harbinger.

Segal, Z. V., Williams, J. M. G., & Teasdale, J. D. (2001). *Mindfulness-based cognitive therapy for depression: A new approach to preventing relapse.* New York: Guilford Press.

Weissman, M. M. (2005). *Mastering depression through interpersonal psychotherapy: Patient workbook.* New York: Oxford University Press.

➤ For more information on the empirical support for these treatments, clinical training materials, and training opportunities, please see www.psychologicaltreatments.org.

➤ The Web site www.therapyadvisor.com provides descriptions, references to empirical support, clinical training materials, and training opportunities for many of the empirically supported treatments (ESTs) identified by the original Division 12 review groups.

5

How Do You Integrate Empirically Supported Treatments into Treatment Planning?

Construction of an empirically informed treatment plan for depression involves integrating objectives and treatment interventions consistent with identified empirically supported treatments (ESTs) into a client's treatment plan after you have determined that the client's primary problem fits those described in the target population of the EST research. Of course, implementing ESTs must be done in consideration of important client, therapist, and therapeutic relationship factors—consistent with the definition of evidence-based practice.

Definitions

The behavioral definition statements describe *how the problem manifests itself in the client*. Although there are several common features of depression, the behavioral definition of depression for your client will be unique and specific to him or her. Your assessment will need to identify which features best characterize your client's presentation. Accordingly, the *behavioral definition* of your treatment plan is tailored to your individual client's clinical picture. When the primary problem reflects a recognized psychiatric diagnosis, the behavioral definition statements are usually closely aligned with diagnostic criteria, such as those provided in the DSM or ICD. Examples of common depression definition statements are the following:

- Persistently depressed or irritable mood
- Diminished interest in or enjoyment of activities
- Social withdrawal
- Feelings of hopelessness, worthlessness, or inappropriate guilt
- Lack of energy or fatigue
- Poor concentration and indecisiveness
- Loss of appetite and/or weight
- Psychomotor agitation or retardation
- Insomnia or hypersomnia

➣ Suicidal thoughts and/or gestures

➣ Low self-esteem

➣ Unresolved grief issues

➣ History of depression for which the client has taken antidepressant medication, been hospitalized, had outpatient treatment, or had a course of electroconvulsive therapy

➣ Others

Goals

Goals are broad statements describing what you and the client would like the result of therapy to be. One statement may suffice, but more than one can be used in the treatment plan. Examples of common goal statements for depression are the following:

➣ Alleviate depressed mood and return to previous level of effective functioning

➣ Recognize, accept, and cope with feelings of depression

➣ Develop healthy and adaptive cognitive patterns and beliefs about self, others, the world, and the future that lead to alleviation and help prevent the relapse of depression

➣ Develop healthy and adaptive interpersonal relationships that lead to alleviation and help prevent the relapse of depression symptoms

➣ Appropriately grieve the loss in order to normalize mood and to return to previous adaptive level of functioning

➣ Others

Objectives and Interventions

Objectives are statements that describe *small, observable steps the client must achieve* toward attaining the goal of successful treatment. Intervention statements describe the *actions taken by the therapist* to assist the client in achieving his/her objectives. Each objective must be paired with at least one intervention.

Assessment

All approaches to quality treatment start with a thorough assessment of the nature and history of the client's presenting problems. EST approaches to treatment rely on a thorough psychosocial assessment of the nature, history, and severity of the problem as experienced by the client.

Table 5.1 contains examples of assessment objectives and interventions for depression.

Table 5.1   Assessment Objectives and Interventions

Objectives	Interventions
1. Describe current and past experiences with depression complete with its impact on function and attempts to resolve it.	1. Assess current and past mood episodes including their features, frequency, intensity, and duration.
2. Verbally identify, if possible, the source of depressed mood.	1. Assist the client in making a list of what he/she is depressed about; refine toward identifying primary cognitive, behavioral, interpersonal, or other contributors. 2. Encourage the client to share his/her thoughts and feelings of depression, identifying primary cognitive, behavioral, interpersonal, or other contributors.
3. Complete psychological testing to assess the depth of depression, the need for antidepressant medication, and suicide prevention measures.	1. Arrange for the administration of an objective assessment instrument for evaluating the client's depression and suicide risk; identifying primary cognitive, behavioral, interpersonal, or other contributors; give feedback to the client if clinically useful.
4. Verbalize any history of suicide attempts and any current suicidal urges.	1. Assess the client's history and current state of suicidal urges and behavior. 2. Assess and monitor the client's suicide potential. 3. Arrange for hospitalization, as necessary, if the client is judged to be harmful to self.
5. Keep a daily journal of depressive symptoms, including the situations in which they occurred and thoughts, feelings, and actions associated with them.	1. Assign the client to keep a daily record of depressive symptoms, including their intensity (e.g., using Subjective Units of Distress [SUDs], the situations in which they occurred, and thoughts, feelings, and actions associated with them.

Psychoeducation

A typical feature of many ESTs for depression is initial and ongoing psychoeducation. A common emphasis is helping the client learn about depression, the treatment, and its rationale. Often, books or other reading material are recommended to the client to supplement psychoeducation done in session. It is important to instill hope in the client and have them on board as a partner in the treatment process. With ESTs, discussing their demonstrated efficacy with the client can facilitate this.

Table 5.2 contains examples of psychoeducational objectives and interventions for depression.

Table 5.2   Psychoeducational Objectives and Interventions

Objectives	Interventions
6. Verbalize an accurate understanding of depression.	1. Discuss how cognitive, behavioral, interpersonal, and/or other factors (e.g., family history) contribute to depression. 2. Assign the client to read psychoeducational chapters of books or treatment manuals on depression.
7. Verbalize an understanding of the rationale for treatment of depression.	1. Discuss how cognitive, behavioral, or interpersonal change can help clients alleviate depression and return to previous level of effective functioning. 2. Assign the client to read about cognitive, behavioral, or interpersonal therapy in chapters of books or treatment manuals on depression.

Cognitive Restructuring

Many of the ESTs for depression include objectives and interventions designed to help the client identify, challenge, and change biased, depressogenic thoughts that support depression. The clinician may use discussion in the session, Socratic questioning, or review of journal material focused on daily thinking patterns to bring to light examples of the client's depressive thoughts that need to be revised and replaced. Assignments are often given to clients to ask them to "test" their biased thoughts against the reality of daily life. These are referred to as *behavioral experiments*.

Much of the therapist's effort is focused on facilitating the client's shift from depressive self-talk to more reality-based, adaptive messages, and then reinforcing the client's efforts and progress toward accomplishing that objective. Later therapy may explore and restructure underlying assumptions and beliefs reflected in biased self-talk that may put the client at risk for relapse or recurrence.

Key Points

The primary steps in the cognitive restructuring procedure can be summarized as follows:

1. Teach the connection between thoughts and feelings.
2. Help clients learn to identify their negatively biased appraisals.
3. Challenge the negatively biased thought patterns.
4. Assist the client in generating reality-based alternatives that correct for the biases.
5. Assign behavioral experiment homework to help reinforce more reality-based appraisals.
6. Reinforce the client's shift from distorted, negative self-talk to more positive, adaptive self-talk.
7. Make and reinforce the connection between positive thought changes and improved mood.

Table 5.3 contains examples of an objective and interventions that show how cognitive restructuring can be described in a treatment plan for depression.

Table 5.3   Cognitive Restructuring Objective and Interventions

Objectives	Interventions
8. Identify, challenge, and change biased self-talk supporting depression.	1. Assist the client in developing an awareness of the connection between cognition and depressive feeling and action. 2. Assign the client to keep a daily journal of automatic thoughts associated with depressive feelings; process the journal material to identify biases; develop alternatives that correct for the biases. 3. Assign "behavioral experiments" in which depressive automatic thoughts are treated as hypotheses/predictions and tested against alternative hypotheses/predictions that correct for the depressive biases. 4. Facilitate and reinforce the client's shift from biased depressive self-talk and beliefs to reality-based cognitive messages that enhance self-confidence and increase adaptive actions. 5. Explore and restructure underlying assumptions and beliefs reflected in biased self-talk that may put the client at risk for relapse or recurrence.

Demonstration Vignette

Cognitive Restructuring

Here we present the transcript of the dialogue depicted in the cognitive restructuring vignette.

Therapist: So Maria, how has the breakup with Carlos affected you? What have you been feeling?

Client: I'm so sad. I've been so depressed. I cry all the time. I'm lonely. I don't think I can make it on my own.

Therapist: Just a great deal of sadness and just being overwhelmed right now. I know this has been a very sad time for you. Any other feelings beyond sad and lonely?

Client: Yeah, at the same time I'm so angry with Carlos. He was such a liar and fake. I'm angry with myself. I'm so stupid for getting into this relationship in the first place. I didn't have to. Why did this have to happen to me? It's not even fair.

Therapist: So the sadness and the loneliness, but then angry at him and even angry at yourself. In previous sessions we talked about how messages we give ourselves—we called them self-talk—trigger emotional reactions. Thoughts influence feelings, so if you can identify the thoughts that are behind the feelings, then you can evaluate them to see if they are reasonable and realistic. If you change the thoughts, you change the feelings. Now in the past, we've seen that your thoughts are very heavily biased in the negative direction. But if you change the thoughts triggered by an event, then you can also alter the feelings, too. So, let's look at the connections between your thoughts and your feelings. You said you are feeling angry and depressed, right?

Client: Exactly. I can hardly get up in the morning to go to work.

Therapist: What's going on there for you? Let's identify some of the thoughts that have accompanied those feelings. You said Carlos was a liar and a fake, right?

(continues)

Client:	Right.
Therapist:	So that's one of the thoughts triggering the angry feelings. As we said, we want to make sure we examine these thoughts and perhaps challenge them if they aren't really working for you. Let me ask you, you would agree that Carlos wasn't all bad?
Client:	No, he has some good qualities.
Therapist:	Of course he did. Can you see that just labeling him in a globally negative way not only makes you angry, but really just isn't true?
Client:	Yeah. Is that on the list, that list of thinking errors we talked about?
Therapist:	[Smiling] Yes. Overgeneralizing, also called polarizing. It's the tendency to see it in black or white terms.
Client:	Yeah, I guess I'm doing that.
Therapist:	So what would be a more realistic way to talk about Carlos that's probably more complex and not simply black and white, not all good or all bad?
Client:	I don't know. He had some good qualities.
Therapist:	He had some good qualities that attracted you.
Client:	Yeah. And he had some bad ones, too.
Therapist:	He had some negative qualities that just turned you off.
Client:	Carlos was good to me sometimes and I think that's why I miss him. But now I see things that tell me to stay away from him, to back off.
Therapist:	Good. How does it feel to be thinking of it like that?
Client:	Actually, it makes me feel a little calmer, a little more, I don't know, in balance maybe.
Therapist:	You see how this works?
Client:	Yeah, I do.
Therapist:	Let's look at some of the other self-talk and how these feelings are connected.
Client:	Okay.

Critique of the Cognitive Restructuring Demonstration Vignette

The following points were made in the critique:

➤ Therapist tied client's thoughts to feelings
➤ Therapist identified thoughts tied to depressive feelings and helped generate alternative, adaptive thoughts
➤ Therapist and client began to identify some underlying biases ("thinking errors") in client's thinking
➤ This process normally takes several sessions
➤ Therapist attended to and reflected client's affect

Additional points that could be made:

➤ Considerable psychoeducation is usually necessary to help the client see the connection between thoughts and feelings as well understand the concept of biased thinking patterns (or thinking errors)

➤ The therapist could assign homework that involves journaling the biased thinking patterns.

Comments you would like to make:

_____

_____

_____

_____

Homework: The exercise "Negative Thoughts Trigger Negative Feelings" is an example of an intervention consistent with cognitive therapy, and designed to help educate the client about biased thinking and its impact on emotions (see www.wiley .com/go/depressionwb). This assignment also provides an opportunity for the client to examine her thinking in response to events in her life and begin to develop positive, reality-based replacement thoughts. Additional homework exercises consistent with cognitive restructuring are "Positive Self Talk," "Journal and Replace Self-Defeating Thoughts," and "Journal of Distorted, Negative Thoughts" (see www. wiley.com/go/depressionwb).

Cognitive Structuring Review

1. What are the primary steps involved in cognitive restructuring?

Cognitive Structuring Review Test Questions

1. In cognitive restructuring, clients are asked to examine thoughts, appraisals, and/or predictions that may be biased toward depression against alternatives that correct for the bias through real life exercises designed to test the two. These exercises are called:

   A. Behavioral experiments
   B. Conflict resolution experiments
   C. Exposure experiments
   D. Problem-solving experiments

2. One of the first steps in cognitive restructuring for depression is to:

   A. Assign behavioral experiment homework to help reinforce more reality-based appraisals

   B. Assist the client in generating reality-based alternatives that correct for the biases

   C. Challenge the negatively biased thought patterns

   D. Teach the connection between thoughts and feelings

Behavioral Activation

Behavioral therapies commonly use techniques such as skills training and activity scheduling to increase engagement in potentially rewarding experiences through which the client derives pleasure, a sense of mastery, purpose, and other positively reinforcing and otherwise antidepressant emotions. Skills are typically taught that help the client maximize opportunities for deriving reward through activities.

Behavioral activation, in particular, has shown a powerfully positive impact on depression. Behavioral activation uses activity scheduling to increase the client's engagement in activities that have a high likelihood of providing pleasure and reward.

Key Points

The primary steps in the behavioral activation procedure can be summarized as:
1. Assess current activities.
2. Identify pleasurable activities in each of the three types of categories.
3. Create a behavioral activation schedule.
4. Prescribe activities through homework exercises.
5. Review homework, reinforcing success, and problem-solving obstacles.
6. Highlight the mood improvement that accompanies increased activity.
7. Repeat.

Three categories of activities are emphasized for inclusion because of their particularly strong connection to mood, as noted by Lewinsohn and colleagues (Lewinsohn, Munoz, Youngren, & Zeiss, 1986):

1. Positive social interactions (e.g., spending time with a good friend)
2. Activities that make one feel useful (e.g., caring for one's child, doing a job well)
3. Activities that are intrinsically pleasant (e.g., a meal at one's favorite restaurant, listening to music)

Table 5.4 contains an example of an objective and treatment interventions describing the use of behavioral strategies, including behavioral activation.

Table 5.4   Behavioral Strategy Objective and Interventions

Objective	Interventions
9. Utilize behavioral strategies to overcome depression.	1. Engage the client in *behavioral activation*, increasing the client's contact with sources of reward, identifying processes that inhibit activation, and teaching skills to solve life problems; use behavioral techniques such as instruction, rehearsal, role-playing, and role-reversal, as needed, to assist adoption in the client's daily life; reinforce success. 2. Assist the client in developing skills that increase the likelihood of deriving pleasure from behavioral activation (e.g., assertiveness skills, developing an exercise plan, less internal/more external focus, increased social involvement); reinforce success.

Demonstration Vignette

Behavioral Activation

Here we present the transcript of the dialogue depicted in the behavioral activation vignette.

Therapist: Have you gotten out much to be with friends, or to do some of your volunteer work at Big Sisters, or just do things like walking around in the mall like you used to?

Client: No, I haven't felt like doing anything. I just don't seem to have the energy.

Therapist: You know, as we have been discussing, one of the things you can do to lift depression is to increase your level of activity. Being more active can help you to increase your general sense of pleasure, help you feel more useful, and build your confidence. I know it's difficult to get moving again, but I'd like you to try to start with very small activities and build up to some more ambitious projects. Do you think you can try that?

Client: I'm not sure.

(continues)

Therapist: Well, I know some of the things you enjoyed doing in the past, but I want you to look at this list. It's over 100 different pleasurable things you can do to help get yourself moving. I want you to look it over, take it home, and complete a homework assignment with them.

[Fade out as they start to look over the list]

NEXT SESSION

Therapist: Did you pick some of the activities out from the list for your homework assignment?

Client: I did, but it was tough. It took a lot of energy just to work on it. But it did remind me of some things I used to enjoy doing.

Therapist: Okay, great. I'm glad that you did that. Let's pick out just three activities that we can focus on. How about we take one from each category. So first, the Positive Social Interactions category. What did you write down for that?

Client: I wrote down going to the movies with my sister. She keeps asking me to go to the movies with her. We used to have fun doing that. We always liked that.

Therapist: Perfect. Now how about an activity from the Useful Events category? What did you put there?

Client: I picked organizing my closet and drawers. I keep putting that on the side, maybe because they are always messy and I don't want to put up with that.

Therapist: That's another good choice. Now, what did you have in the category of Intrinsically Pleasant Activities? Those are the things that are just fun to do.

Client: I picked getting my hair done and just interacting with the people in the salon. I always love it when people make me feel pretty, and when I get my hair and my nails done it makes me feel pretty.

Therapist: Very good. Let's look at your schedule for this week and see what you could commit to doing.

Client: All right.

Critique of the Behavioral Activation Demonstration Vignette

The following points were made in the critique:

➤ Therapist builds a solid rationale for the behavioral activation procedure

➤ Resistance to increased activity is expected, so start with a simple activity first

➤ Therapist structures the identified activities around Lewinsohn's three categories

➤ With sensitivity to compliance issues, the therapist works with the client to specifically schedule this activity into the next week

Additional points that could be made:

➤ Rationale building will probably take more time than depicted in the demo

➤ Homework was used very constructively in this demonstration

➤ Therapist regularly used positive reinforcement in response to the client's completion of the homework

➤ Therapist might tie the activity to a mood journal to connect improvement in feelings to increased activity

➤ Rehearsal could be used to problem-solve any obstacles to implementing the activity and to increase compliance motivation

Comments you would like to make:

_____

_____

_____

_____

Homework: The exercise "Identify and Schedule Pleasant Activities" is an example of an intervention consistent with behavioral activation (see www.wiley.com/go/depressionwb).

Often, this exercise must be accompanied by processing the client's resistance to initiating activity. If the client does not follow through with selecting activities on her own, a session or two may have to be devoted to this process, with the therapist helping to move the procedure forward. Role-play and role-reversal may be helpful as an intermediate step to helping the client implement activity in real life. Following up with a review of the assigned activity is essential. It allows the therapist to reinforce success, and its positive effect on mood, and to problem-solve any identified obstacles.

Behavioral Activation Review

1. What are the primary steps involved in behavioral activation?

Behavioral Activation Review Test Questions

1. Which of the following is NOT one of the three types of activities thought to have a particularly strong connection to mood and often emphasized in behavioral activation?

   A. Activities that are intrinsically pleasant
   B. Activities that make one feel useful
   C. Positive social interactions
   D. Responsibilities that have been avoided

2. One of the first steps in behavioral activation for depression is to:
   A. Assess current activities
   B. Create a behavioral activation schedule
   C. Identify pleasurable activities in each of the three types of categories
   D. Prescribe activities through homework exercises

Behavioral Activation Reference

Lewinsohn, P. M., Munoz, R., Youngren, M., & Zeiss, A. M. (1986). *Control your depression*. NY: Fireside.

Personal and Interpersonal Skills Training and Problem-Solving

Nearly every identified EST for depression includes skills training to help improve the quality and satisfaction derived from interpersonal interaction. Examples of common skills trained include conversational and assertive communication skills, problem-solving and decision-making skills, and conflict resolution skills. These skills are often taught to the client, practiced in session, and then assigned through homework exercises. In some cases, conjoint sessions may be used. In this subsection we highlight problem-solving skills training.

Primary Emphases in Problem-Solving Therapy

Problem-solving therapy, or PST, teaches patients to more effectively approach and resolve problems in their lives. Through PST, clients learn to understand and change the nature of their problems, their reactions to them, or both, using a *positive problem orientation* and *problem-solving skills.*

> A positive problem orientation refers to a motivational technique that helps clients understand that it is *normal* to have problems and that they can resolve them effectively by facing and solving them.
> Clients also learn the steps for effective problem-solving skills and how to use them with current problems in living.
>   1. Define the problem specifically.
>   2. Generate options for addressing the problem without evaluating them.
>   3. Evaluate the pros and cons of the generated solution options.
>   4. Select the best solution and implement it.
>   5. Evaluate the effectiveness of the plan.
>   6. Keep, revise, or change the plan based on the evaluation of its effectiveness.

Table 5.5 contains examples of objectives and interventions consistent with skills training, including problem-solving.

Table 5.5   Skills Training Objectives and Interventions

Objectives	Interventions
10. Learn and implement assertive communication skills.	1. Use techniques such as psychoeducation, modeling, and role-playing to teach client assertiveness skills; assign homework exercises; review and repeat toward improving the goal integrating their use into the client's life.
11. Learn and implement problem-solving and decision-making skills.	1. Use techniques such as psychoeducation, modeling, and role-playing to teach client problem-solving skills, including defining problems, generating possible solutions, evaluating solutions, developing a plan, implementing the plan, evaluating the efficacy of the plan, and accepting or revising the plan.
	2. Help the client resolve depression related to interpersonal problems through the use of reassurance and support, clarification of cognitive and affective triggers that ignite conflicts, and active problem-solving.
12. Learn and implement conflict resolution skills to resolve interpersonal problems.	1. Teach conflict resolution skills (e.g., empathy, active listening, "I messages," respectful communication, assertiveness without aggression, compromise); use psychoeducation, modeling, role-playing, and rehearsal to work through several current conflicts; assign homework exercises; review and repeat toward improving the goal integrating their use into the client's life.
13. Participate in conjoint sessions to address interpersonal problems.	1. In conjoint sessions, help the client resolve interpersonal conflicts using interpersonal skills such as assertion, problem-solving, and conflict resolution.

Demonstration Vignette

Problem-Solving Skills

Here we provide the transcript of the dialogue depicted in the problem-solving vignette.

(continues)

Therapist:	You have mentioned your frustration over conflicts with Sue at work. What's the issue there?
Client:	I get so frustrated. She's nasty.
Therapist:	Okay, so let's approach this as we've discussed before. The first step is to define the problem specifically. Let's try that. Tell me how she's nasty. Think of specific examples.
Client:	Well, she ignores me every time I say good morning to her. Her desk is right next to mine. She even looks away when I look at her. Plus she's always late for work.
Therapist:	Okay, let's take these one at a time. It sounds like one issue is the morning greeting problem, so what are your options to deal with this?
Client:	I guess I could just keep saying hello and being polite to her and see if there's any changes.
Therapist:	So that's one option. Just keep doing what you are doing. How about others?
Client:	I could stop saying hello and just ignore her like she's ignoring me. Or I could always tell her off.
Therapist:	Those are two other options. Others?
Client:	I'm not sure.
Therapist:	How about talking to her in a way that shares how her behavior makes you feel sad and hurt?
Client:	I guess. Doesn't she know that?
Therapist:	Can you assume she does?
Client:	I guess not. Maybe she doesn't.
Therapist:	Okay, let's go to the next step. Let's look at our four options and consider the pros and cons of each. The first option was to just keep on doing what you are doing. What are the pros and cons there?
Client:	Well, it could frustrate me even more. I have been doing this for weeks, so no, I don't think that's going to work.
Therapist:	So, more of the same, just longer. What about option two—ignoring her?
Client:	That might lower some of my frustration, but it also might make the tension between us even bigger.
Therapist:	Less frustration, but more tension. I see what you're saying. How about confronting her with your anger about her behavior—just "telling her off"?
Client:	I think I'd feel better.
Therapist:	Any cons or any drawbacks to this?
Client:	Well, I might feel better for a little while, but I think that would probably just make her mad and cause a bigger frustration or bigger problem between us.
Therapist:	How about the option of sharing your feelings in a non-confrontational, non-aggressive manner, telling her how her behavior hurts your feelings. What's the downside or the benefits of this?
Client:	Well, it may take her by surprise if I tell her that I'm hurt, or she could mock me, but maybe it would start us talking, start talking to each other.
Therapist:	So are you getting a sense for the best option for you?
Client:	Yeah, talking to her would probably be better.
Therapist:	Okay, good. So let's role-play how you might say this to her.

> Client: Okay. I'm not sure if I can do this right. "Sue, I want to tell you something important. I feel so hurt when I say hello or good morning to you and you don't respond back to me. That makes me feel bad."
>
> Therapist: I think that is excellent. You were not accusatory, but you were clear about your feelings. Now let's take it the next step further. Let's work on how you can follow this by discussing with her how the situation might be made better. Are you ready?
>
> Client: Yes. "Sue, I want to tell you something important. . . ."

Critique of the Problem–Solving Demonstration Vignette

The following points were made in the critique:

➤ Therapist helped the client specify the definition of the problem, what "nasty" meant to her, which facilitates better problem-solving

➤ Good leading of the client to generate options for solution to problem

➤ Cognitive restructuring can be used in conjunction with the problem-solving technique to examine exaggeration or black-and-white thinking

➤ Therapist proposes the constructive option of sharing feelings non-aggressively; in later sessions it would be helpful to lead the client to generate this option

➤ Therapist helps the client examine pros and cons of each option

Additional points that could be made:

➤ More time could be spent looking at the pros and cons of each option

➤ Good use of rehearsal but increased role-play by the therapist as the coworker might have been helpful

➤ Scheduling the implementation is important and then following up to problem-solve or reinforce success

Comments you would like to make:

_____

_____

_____

_____

Homework: The homework exercise "Applying Problem-Solving to Interpersonal Conflict" is an example of an intervention consistent with problem-solving (see www.wiley.com/go/depressionwb).

Problem-Solving Therapy Review

1. What are the two primary emphases of problem-solving therapy?
2. What is a positive problem orientation?
3. What are the primary steps involved in solving a problem?

Problem-Solving Therapy Review Test Questions

1. When conceptualizing a problem to be subjected to problem-solving, it is important to:

    A. Define it in specific terms
    B. First determine whether it is solvable
    C. Make sure it is tied to social interaction
    D. Simultaneously think of options for solving it

2. The concept of a positive problem orientation refers to which of the following?

    A. A manner of defining problems that frames them in a positive way
    B. A motivational technique that encourages clients to accept and solve problems
    C. A set of steps used to solve problems
    D. A process used when a problem-solving plan fails

Interpersonal Therapy (IPT)

Interpersonal therapy (IPT) treats depression in its interpersonal context. Accordingly, initial sessions are devoted to taking a detailed *interpersonal inventory* of important past and present relationships and formulating the patient's depression in interpersonal terms. Emphasis is placed on overcoming interpersonal loss and grief; resolving interpersonal disputes; transitioning out of old and into new interpersonal roles; and developing new or more effective interpersonal skills.

The therapeutic techniques used in interpersonal therapy include:

➤ Clarification
➤ Supportive listening
➤ Encouragement of affect
➤ Role-playing
➤ Communication analysis

Table 5.6 contains examples of objectives and interventions consistent with IPT.

Table 5.6   Interpersonal Therapy Objectives and Interventions

Objectives	Interventions
14. Identify important people in your life, past and present, and describe the quality, good and bad, of those relationships.	1. Assess the client's *interpersonal inventory* of important past and present relationships and develop a case formulation linking depression to grief, interpersonal role disputes, role transitions, and/or interpersonal deficits.
15. Participate in therapy toward the goals of understanding and solving the current interpersonal problems.	1. For grief, facilitate mourning and gradually help the client find new activities and relationships to compensate for the loss. 2. For disputes, help the client explore the relationship, the nature of the dispute, whether it has reached an impasse, and available options to resolve it; if the relationship has reached an impasse, consider ways to change the impasse or to end the relationship. 3. For role transitions (e.g., beginning or ending a relationship or career, moving, promotion, retirement, graduation), help the client mourn the loss of the old role while recognizing positive and negative aspects of the new role, and taking steps to gain mastery over the new role. 4. For interpersonal deficits, help the client develop new interpersonal skills and relationships.

Homework: Although the assignment of homework is not a typical feature in interpersonal therapy, the following exercises may be helpful in understanding common interpersonal interventions and may be clinically useful as well: "Creating a Memorial Collage"; "Dear _____: A Letter to a Lost Loved One"; "How Can We Meet Each Other's Needs and Desires"; or "Positive and Negative Contributions to the Relationship: Yours and Mine" (see www.wiley.com/go/depressionwb).

Interpersonal Therapy Review

1. What is an *interpersonal inventory*?
2. What are themes, areas of focus, in IPT?
3. What therapeutic techniques are commonly used in IPT?

Interpersonal Therapy Review Test Questions

1. One of the first steps in interpersonal therapy is to:

   A. Build interpersonal skills
   B. Do a detailed assessment of important past and present relationships
   C. Address grief
   D. Confront defenses

2. Which of the following is a theme common to IPT for depression?

   A. Addressing grief and loss
   B. Challenging cognitive biases
   C. Changing environmental reinforcements
   D. Increasing pleasurable activities

Other Common Approaches to Treatment

Therapists working with depression have also commonly used other approaches that may be part of an overall treatment plan. Examples include:

➤ Probing unexpressed anger ("anger turned inward")
➤ Exploring an abuse history in the family
➤ Enhancing motivation through stage of change interventions
➤ Prescribing or referring for antidepressant medication

CHAPTER 6

What Are Considerations for Relapse Prevention?

Whether treated pharmacologically, psychologically, or both, depression is prone to relapse. There has been some promising work developing formal relapse prevention programs for depression, some of which have received empirical support. Before reviewing those, let's take a look at some common considerations in relapse prevention interventions and how they can be incorporated into your treatment plan.

1. *Explain the rationale for relapse prevention interventions.*

    One of the first steps in relapse prevention interventions is to provide a rationale for them. This typically involves a discussion of the risk for relapse and how using the relapse prevention approach we will outline can lower that risk.

2. *Distinguish between lapse and relapse.*

    ➤ A lapse is presented as a rather common, temporary setback, may involve, for example, re-experiencing a depressive thought and/or urge to withdraw or avoid (perhaps as related to some loss or conflict).

    ➤ Relapse, on the other hand, is described as a return to a sustained pattern of depressive thinking and feeling, usually accompanied by interpersonal withdrawal and/or avoidance.

3. *Identify high-risk situations for a lapse.*

    High-risk situations that might make the client vulnerable to a lapse are identified. This discussion may be informed by past difficult experiences or anticipated new ones. Some examples include:

    ➤ Having an interpersonal conflict after having not had one for some time.

    ➤ Deciding not to use an assertive approach in a situation and then self-deprecating.

    ➤ Having a stressful day, week, or other period and starting to contemplate old depressive thoughts, feelings, and actions.

4. *Review the application of skills learned in therapy to high-risk situations.*

For the high-risk situations identified, the therapist leads the client in a rehearsal of using skills learned in therapy to manage them, including the skills of developing a tolerance for occasional depressive thoughts and feelings while working on how to begin problem-solving them.

5. *Encourage the routine use of skills learned in therapy* (e.g., cognitive restructuring, problem-solving, behavioral activation), instructing the client to build these skills them into his/her life as much as possible.

In addition to using skills learned in therapy to manage high-risk situations, clients are also encouraged to integrate positive thinking, communicating, problem-solving, and staying active into their day-to-day lives.

6. *Consider developing a coping card* that outlines coping strategies and other important information (e.g., steps in problem-solving, reminders regarding assertive communication).

Sometimes clients benefit from having a reminder of important strategies and information regarding relapse prevention.

7. *Schedule periodic booster therapy sessions* to help the client maintain therapeutic gains and problem-solve challenges.

Periodic booster sessions of therapy can help prevent relapse of depression, so clients are invited to periodically revisit therapy to strengthen and reinforce their new approach to life.

Key Points

COMMON CONSIDERATIONS IN RELAPSE PREVENTION

1. Explain the rationale of relapse prevention interventions
2. Distinguish between lapse and relapse
3. Identify high-risk situations for a lapse
4. Review the application of skills learned in therapy to high-risk situations
5. Encourage routine use of skills learned in therapy
6. Consider developing a coping card
7. Schedule periodic booster therapy sessions

Formal Relapse Prevention Interventions for Depression

Some interventions focused directly on relapse prevention, derived from cognitive and cognitive behavioral therapies, have received some empirical support.

Mindfulness-Based Cognitive Therapy

This approach combines mindfulness meditation with cognitive therapy techniques. It helps clients learn to recognize the negative thought processes associated with depression and to change their relationship with these thoughts. MBCT has empirical support for its ability to reduce the risk of relapse in those with chronic depression (see Segal, Williams, & Teasdale, 2001).

Well-Being Therapy

This approach is designed to facilitate well-being after recovery from depression to reduce the risk of relapse. The therapy focuses less on symptom management and more on building strengths that foster mental health (see Fava & Riuni, 2003).

Cognitive Therapy Continuation

This intervention represents a continuation of cognitive therapy after the acute (active) phase of treatment is completed. In it, clients learn to use emotional distress and depressive symptoms to practice the coping and other skills learned during active therapy and to generalize these skills to everyday life (see Jarrett & Kraft, 1997).

EMPIRICALLY SUPPORTED INTERVENTIONS FOR RELAPSE PREVENTION OF DEPRESSION
- Mindfulness-based cognitive therapy
- Well-being therapy
- Cognitive therapy-continuation

For more information about these relapse prevention interventions for depression, see the Web site of The Society of Clinical Psychology (APA Division 12) at www.PsychologicalTreatments.org.

Chapter Review

1. What are the seven common considerations in relapse prevention?

Chapter Review Test Question

1. John and his therapist identify situations that John fears could potentially set him back, should he encounter one. They plan to review these encounters and develop a plan for coping with them. Which consideration in relapse prevention is being used in this example?

   A. Developing a coping card
   B. Distinguishing between lapse and relapse
   C. Encouraging routine use of skills learned in therapy
   D. Identifying high-risk situations for a lapse

Chapter References

Empirical Support

Fava, G. A. (1999). Well-being therapy. *Psychotherapy and Psychosomatics, 68*, 171–178.

Hollon, S. D., DeRubeis, R. J., Shelton, R. C., Amsterdam, J. D., Saloman, R. M., O'Reardon, J. P., et al., (2005). Prevention of relapse following cognitive therapy vs. medications in moderate to severe depression. *Archives of General Psychiatry, 62*, 417–422.

Jarrett, R. D., Kraft, D., Doyle, D., Foster, B. M., Eaves, G. G., & Silver, P. C. (2001). Preventing recurrent depression using cognitive therapy with and without a continuation phase: A randomized clinical trial. *Archives of General Psychiatry, 58*, 381–388.

Ma, S. H., & Teasdale, J. D. (2004). Mindfulness-based cognitive therapy for depression: Replication and exploration of differential relapse prevention effects. *Journal of Consulting and Clinical Psychology, 72*, 31–40.

Teasdale, J. D., Segal, Z. V., Williams, J. M. G., Ridgeway, V. A., Soulsby, J. M., & Lau, M. A. (2000). Prevention of relapse/recurrence in major depression by mindfulness-based cognitive therapy. *Journal of Consulting and Clinical Psychology, 68*, 615–623.

Vittengl, J. R., Clark, L.A., Dunn, T. W., & Jarrett, R. B. (2007). Reducing relapse and recurrence in unipolar depression: A comparative meta-analysis of cognitive-behavioral therapy's effects. *Journal of Consulting and Clinical Psychology, 75*, 475–488.

Clinical Resources

Fava, G., & Riuni, C. (2003). Development and characteristics of a well-being enhancing psychotherapeutic strategy: Well-being therapy. *Journal of Behavior Therapy and Experiential Psychiatry, 34*, 45–63.

Jarrett, R. B., & Kraft, D. (1997). Prophylactic cognitive therapy for major depressive disorder. *Journal of Clinical Psychology: In session, 3*, 65–79.

Segal, Z., Williams, J., & Teasdale, J. (2001) *Mindfulness based cognitive therapy for depression: A new approach to preventing relapse.* New York: Guilford Press.

Bibliotherapy Resource

Williams, J., Teasdale, J., Segal, Z., & Kabat-Zinn, J. (2007). *The mindful way through depression: Freeing yourself from chronic unhappiness.* New York: Guilford Press.

Closing Remarks and Resources

As we note on the DVD, it is important to be aware that the research support for any particular empirically supported treatment (EST) supports the identified treatment as it was delivered in the studies supporting it. The use of only selected objectives or interventions from ESTs may not be empirically supported.

If you want to incorporate an EST into your treatment plan, it should reflect the major objectives and interventions of the approach. Note that in addition to their primary objectives and interventions, many ESTs have options within them that may or may not be used depending on the client's need (e.g., skills training).

Most treatment manuals, books, and other training programs identify the primary objectives and interventions used in the EST. Of course, in accordance with ethical guidelines, therapists should have competency in the services they deliver.

An existing resource for integrating research-supported treatments into treatment planning is the Practice*Planner*® series[1] of *Treatment Planners*. The series contains several books that have integrated goals, objectives, and interventions consistent with those of identified ESTs into treatment plans for several applicable problems and disorders:

➢ *The Severe and Persistent Mental Illness Treatment Planner* (Berghuis, Jongsma, & Bruce).
➢ *The Family Therapy Treatment Planner* (Dattilio, Jongsma, & Davis)
➢ *The Complete Adult Psychotherapy Treatment Planner* (Jongsma, Peterson, & Bruce)
➢ *The Adolescent Psychotherapy Treatment Planner* (Jongsma, Peterson, McInnis, & Bruce).

---

[1]These books are updated frequently, check with the publisher for the latest editions, and information about the Practice*Planner*® series.

> *The Child Psychotherapy Treatment Planner* (Jongsma, Peterson, McInnis & Bruce).
> *The Veterans and Active Duty Military Psychotherapy Treatment Planner* (Moore & Jongsma)
> *The Addiction Treatment Planner* (Perkinson, Jongsma, & Bruce)
> *The Couples Psychotherapy Treatment Planner* (O'Leary, Heyman, & Jongsma)

Finally, it is important to remember that the purpose of this series is to demonstrate the process of empirically informed psychotherapy treatment planning for common mental health problems. It is designed to be informational in nature and does not intend to be a substitute for clinical training in the interventions discussed and demonstrated. Of course, in accordance with ethical guidelines, therapists should have competency in the services they deliver.

A

Chapter Review Test Question Answers Explained

Chapter 1: What Are the DSM Criteria for Depression?

1. Which of the following meets the criteria for a major depressive episode (MDE), assuming its presence for more than two weeks:

    A. Fatigue, insomnia, withdrawal, loss of appetite, concern about symptoms
    B. Irritability, agitation, argumentativeness, disorganized thinking, impulsivity
    C. Sadness, fatigue, excessive appetite, excessive sleeping, psychomotor slowing
    D. Sadness, anxiety, recent loss of job, insomnia, worry

       A. *Incorrect*: This profile fails to meet the 5-SIGECAPSS criteria for an MDE because "withdrawal" and "concern about symptoms" are not diagnostic criteria. Although withdrawal may or may not reflect the diagnostic feature of "I" (loss of interest), concern about symptoms is not diagnostic.

       B. *Incorrect*: Although irritability can be the prominent mood in depression, this profile does not meet the 5-SIGECAPSS criteria for an MDE and is actually more characteristic of (dysphoric) mania.

       C. *Correct*: This profile meets the 5-SIGECAPSS criteria for an MDE.

       D. *Incorrect*: This profile fails to meet the 5-SIGECAPSS criteria for an MDE. "Recent loss of job" and "anxiety" may precipitate and accompany depression, respectively, but are not diagnostic criteria.

2. A person currently meeting the criteria for an MDE could have which of the following types of mood disorders?

    A. Unipolar
    B. Bipolar
    C. Either unipolar or bipolar
    D. Neither unipolar nor bipolar

A. *Incorrect*: A person with a current MDE may have had past depressive, manic, hypomanic, or mixed episodes, making C the correct answer.

B. *Incorrect*: A person with a current MDE may have had past depressive, manic, hypomanic, or mixed episodes, making C the correct answer.

C. *Correct*: A person with a current MDE may have had past depressive, manic, hypomanic, or mixed episodes, making this the correct answer.

D. *Incorrect*: A person with a current MDE meets criteria for a major depressive disorder and may have had past depressive, manic, hypomanic, or mixed episodes.

Chapter 2: What Are the Six Steps in Building a Treatment Plan?

1. A psychotherapy treatment plan can be drawn up without a diagnosis. For example, a good case formulation can be the basis of therapy. Why is it important to consider the diagnosis when developing a plan that could be informed by empirically supported treatments (ESTs)?

   A. A diagnosis is necessary to judge response to the EST.
   B. It is not necessary to consider diagnosis in empirically informed treatment planning.
   C. Some ESTs were developed and studied using diagnosis as inclusion criteria.
   D. Treatment may require medication, which typically requires diagnosis to be specified.

      A. *Incorrect*: Although diagnostic criteria can be used to assess response to treatment, outcome of treatment can be measured in other ways as well.
      B. *Incorrect*: See C.
      C. *Correct*: Many ESTs were developed for the treatment problems defined by a diagnosis. Knowing the diagnosis is particularly important in deciding whether an EST is applicable to a client.
      D. *Incorrect*: Although diagnosis is important in determining medication choice, this question pertains to ESTs, which are empirically supported psychological treatments.

2. The statement "Identify, challenge, and change biased self-talk supportive of depression" is an example of which of the following steps in a treatment plan?

   A. A primary problem
   B. A short-term objective
   C. A symptom manifestation
   D. A treatment intervention

A. *Incorrect*: The primary problem (Step 1 in treatment planning) is the summary description, usually in diagnostic terms, of the client's primary problem.

B. *Correct*: This is a short-term objective (Step 5 in treatment planning). It describes the desired actions of the client in the treatment plan.

C. *Incorrect*: Symptom manifestations (Step 2 in treatment planning) describe the client's particular expression (i.e., manifestations or symptoms) of a problem.

D. *Incorrect*: A treatment intervention (Step 6 in treatment planning) describes the therapist's actions designed to help the client achieve therapeutic objectives.

Chapter 3: What Is the Brief History of the Empirically Supported Treatments Movement?

1. Which statement best describes the process used to identify ESTs?

   A. Consumers of mental health services nominated therapies.

   B. Experts came to a consensus based on their experiences with the treatments.

   C. Researchers submitted their works.

   D. Task groups reviewed the literature using clearly defined selection criteria for ESTs.

      A. *Incorrect*: Mental health professionals selected ESTs.

      B. *Incorrect*: Expert consensus was not the method used to identify ESTs.

      C. *Incorrect*: Empirical works in the existing literature were reviewed to identify ESTs.

      D. *Correct*: Review groups consisting of mental health professionals selected ESTs based on predetermined criteria.

2. Based on the differences in their criteria, in which of the following ways are well-established treatments different than those classified as probably efficacious?

   A. Only probably efficacious treatments allowed the use of a single case design experiments.

   B. Only well-established treatments allowed studies comparing the treatment to a psychological placebo.

   C. Only well-established treatments required demonstration by at least two different, independent investigators or investigating teams.

   D. Only well-established treatments allowed studies comparing the treatment to a pill placebo.

A. *Incorrect*: Both sets of criteria allowed use of single subject designs. Well-established treatments required a larger series than did probably efficacious treatments (see II under well-established and III under probably efficacious).

B. *Incorrect*: Studies using comparison to psychological placebos were acceptable in both sets of criteria (see IA under well-established and II under probably efficacious).

C. *Correct*: One of the primary differences between treatments classified as well-established and those classified as probably efficacious is that well-established therapies have had their efficacy demonstrated by at least two different, independent investigators (see V under well-established).

D. *Incorrect*: Studies using comparison to pill placebos were acceptable in both sets of criteria (see IA under well-established and II under probably efficacious).

Chapter 4: What Are the Identified Empirically Supported Treatments for Depression?

1. The therapeutic intervention that involves scheduling client activities that increase the clients' exposure to rewarding feelings such as pleasure, feeling worthwhile, productive, and the like is called

   A. Behavioral activation
   B. Behavioral experiment
   C. Behavioral exposure
   D. Behavioral therapy

   A. *Correct*: The question describes behavioral activation.
   B. *Incorrect*: Behavioral experiments involve testing predictions and are used in cognitive restructuring.
   C. *Incorrect*: Although behavioral exposure asks client to engage in activities, *feared* activities are targeted for the purpose of reducing the fear.
   D. *Incorrect*: Behavioral therapy is a term that subsumes several therapeutic interventions including behavioral activation and exposure.

2. The practice of thoroughly assessing important past and present relationships with others is a prominent feature of which EST for depression?

   A. Behavior therapy
   B. Cognitive therapy
   C. Interpersonal therapy
   D. Problem-solving therapy

A. *Incorrect*: Although thorough assessment is emphasized in behavior therapy, an emphasis on important past relationships does not characterize it.

B. *Incorrect*: Although thorough assessment is emphasized in cognitive therapy, an emphasis on important past relationships does not characterize it.

C. *Correct*: The question describes IPT's emphasis on taking an interpersonal inventory of important past and current relationships.

D. *Incorrect*: Although thorough assessment is emphasized in problem-solving therapy, an emphasis on important past relationships does not characterize it.

Chapter 5: How Do You Integrate Empirically Supported Treatments into Treatment Planning?

Cognitive Restructuring

1. In cognitive restructuring, clients are asked to examine thoughts, appraisals, and/or predictions that may be biased toward depression and compare them to alternatives that correct for the bias, through real-life exercises designed to test the two. These exercises are called:

   A. Behavioral experiments
   B. Conflict resolution experiments
   C. Exposure experiments
   D. Problem-solving experiments

      A. *Correct*: The question describes testing of maladaptive versus potentially adaptive cognition through behavioral experiments, a hallmark of cognitive therapy.

      B. *Incorrect*: Conflict resolution refers to a set of skills often trained in behavioral approaches to depression and other problems involving interpersonal conflict.

      C. *Incorrect*: Exposure refers to behavior therapy techniques designed to reduce anxiety through repeated exposure to what is feared.

      D. *Incorrect*: Problem-solving refers to a set of skills and a therapeutic approach to depression that emphasizes a systematic approach to addressing and resolving life problems.

2. One of the first steps in cognitive restructuring for depression is to:

   A. Assign behavioral experiment homework to help reinforce more reality-based appraisals

B. Assist the client in generating reality-based alternatives that correct for the biases
C. Challenge the negatively biased thought patterns
D. Teach the connection between thoughts and feelings
   A. *Incorrect*: This is a latter step in cognitive restructuring, typically occurring after the client has learned the connection between thoughts and feelings, identified the biases in fearful thoughts, challenged them, and generated alternatives that correct for the biases.
   B. *Incorrect*: This step in cognitive restructuring typically occurs after the client has learned the connection between thoughts and feelings, identified the biases in his or her fearful thinking, and challenged them.
   C. *Incorrect*: This step in cognitive restructuring typically occurs after the client has learned the connection between thoughts and feelings and identified the biases in his or her fearful thinking.
   D. *Correct*: Client are typically taught how thoughts influence feelings before identifying the biases in fearful thoughts, challenging them, and generating alternatives to these biased thoughts.

Behavioral Activation

1. Which of the following is NOT one of the three types of activities thought to have a particularly strong connection to mood and often emphasized in behavioral activation?

   A. Activities that are intrinsically pleasant
   B. Activities that make one feel useful
   C. Positive social interactions
   D. Responsibilities that have been avoided
      A. *Incorrect*: This is one of three categories of activities highlighted in behavioral activation approaches as having a strong connection to mood.
      B. *Incorrect*: This is one of three categories of activities highlighted in behavioral activation approaches as having a strong connection to mood.
      C. *Incorrect*: This is one of three categories of activities highlighted in behavioral activation approaches as having a strong connection to mood.
      D. *Correct*: Although avoided responsibilities may elicit changes in mood, most likely a negative in nature, they are not the types of activities emphasized in behavioral activation.

2. One of the first steps in behavioral activation for depression is to:
    A. Assess current activities
    B. Create a behavioral activation schedule
    C. Identify pleasurable activities in each of the three types of categories
    D. Prescribe activities through homework exercises
        A. *Correct*: A thorough assessment of current activities precedes any intervention designed to change them through behavioral activation.
        B. *Incorrect*: This step is completed after the assessment of current activities and the identification of pleasurable activities have been completed.
        C. *Incorrect*: This step takes place after the assessment of current activities and before creating a schedule for activation.
        D. *Incorrect*: This step follows the three preceding steps.

Personal and Interpersonal Skills Training and Problem-Solving

1. When conceptualizing a problem to be subjected to problem-solving, it is important to:
    A. Define it in specific terms
    B. First determine whether it is solvable
    C. Make sure it is tied to social interaction
    D. Simultaneously think of options for solving it
        A. *Correct*: The first step in problem-solving is to define the problem specifically and descriptively.
        B. *Incorrect*: A problem may be solvable or need to be "let go," but that conclusion is drawn after subjecting it to problem-solving, not before.
        C. *Incorrect*: Problem-solving can be used to approach any problem, not just those tied to social interaction.
        D. *Incorrect*: Generating options for solving a problem comes after first defining it.

2. The concept of a positive problem orientation refers to which of the following?
    A. A manner of defining problems that frames them in a positive way
    B. A motivational technique that encourages clients to accept and solve problems
    C. A set of steps used to solve problems
    D. A process used when a problem-solving plan fails

A. *Incorrect*: Defining a problem is one of the steps in the problem-solving technique. The positive problem orientation refers to an acceptance of problems as a natural part of life.

B. *Correct*: The positive problem orientation refers to a motivational technique that encourages clients to accept problems as a natural part of life and approach them with a problem-solving strategy.

C. *Incorrect*: This answer defines problem-solving, not problem orientation.

D. *Incorrect*: When a problem fails, clients are encouraged to revisit the steps of problem-solving. Although a positive problem orientation might motivate the client to do this, doing so is not the process used.

Interpersonal Therapy

1. One of the first steps in interpersonal therapy is to:

    A. Build interpersonal skills
    B. Assess important past and present relationships
    C. Address grief
    D. Confront defenses

    A. *Incorrect*: A thorough assessment of interpersonal relationships is conducted before interventions in interpersonal therapy.

    B. *Correct*: A thorough assessment of interpersonal relationships, called the interpersonal inventory, is conducted before interventions in interpersonal therapy.

    C. *Incorrect*: A thorough assessment of interpersonal relationships is conducted before interventions in interpersonal therapy.

    D. *Incorrect*: A thorough assessment of interpersonal relationships is conducted before interventions in interpersonal therapy.

2. Which of the following is a theme common to IPT for depression?

    A. Addressing grief and loss
    B. Challenging cognitive biases
    C. Changing environmental reinforcements
    D. Increasing pleasurable activities

    A. *Correct*: Addressing grief and loss is a common theme in interpersonal therapy.

    B. *Incorrect*: This emphasis better characterizes a primary theme of cognitive therapy.

C. *Incorrect*: This emphasis better characterizes a primary theme of behavior therapy.

D. *Incorrect*: This emphasis better characterizes a primary theme of behavioral activation.

Chapter 6: What Are Considerations for Relapse Prevention?

1. John and his therapist identify situations that John fears could potentially set him back, should he encounter one. They plan to review these encounters and develop a plan for coping with them. Which consideration in relapse prevention is being used in this example?

A. Developing a coping card
B. Distinguishing between lapse and relapse
C. Encouraging routine use of skills learned in therapy
D. Identifying high-risk situations for a lapse

   A. *Incorrect*: This is a technique used by some clients to help them remember key therapeutic points and strategies outside of therapy.

   B. *Incorrect*: This is a psychoeducational intervention designed in part to help prevent misinterpretation of potentially manageable setbacks as an unmanageable relapse.

   C. *Incorrect*: This intervention is designed to transport skill use into everyday applications, not just ones that represent a higher risk for relapse.

   D. *Correct:* The vignette describes identifying high-risk situations. John and his therapist will then review and develop a plan for managing them.

STUDY PACKAGE
CONTINUING EDUCATION
CREDIT INFORMATION

Evidence-Based Treatment Planning for Depression

Our goal is to provide you with current, accurate and practical information from the most experienced and knowledgeable speakers and authors.

Listed below are the continuing education credit(s) currently available for this self-study package. *Please note: Your state licensing board dictates whether self study is an acceptable form of continuing education. Please refer to your state rules and regulations.*

COUNSELORS: PESI, LLC is recognized by the National Board for Certified Counselors to offer continuing education for National Certified Counselors. Provider #: 5896. We adhere to NBCC Continuing Education Guidelines. This self-study package qualifies for 2.0 contact hours.

SOCIAL WORKERS: PESI, LLC, 1030, is approved as a provider for continuing education by the Association of Social Work Boards, 400 South Ridge Parkway, Suite B, Culpeper, VA 22701. www.aswb.org. Social workers should contact their regulatory board to determine course approval. Course Level: All Levels. Social Workers will receive 2.0 (Clinical) continuing education clock hours for completing this self-study package.

PSYCHOLOGISTS: PESI, LLC is approved by the American Psychological Association to sponsor continuing education for psychologists. PESI, LLC maintains responsibility for these materials and their content. PESI is offering these self-study materials for 2.0 hours of continuing education credit.

ADDICTION COUNSELORS: PESI, LLC is a Provider approved by NAADAC Approved Education Provider Program. Provider #: 366. This self-study package qualifies for 2.0 contact hours.

MARRIAGE & FAMILY THERAPISTS: This activity consists of 2.0 clock hours of continuing education instruction. Credit requirements and approvals vary per state board regulations. Please save the course outline, the certificate of completion you receive from the activity and contact your state board or organization to determine specific filing requirements.

NURSES/NURSE PRACTITIONERS/CLINICAL NURSE SPECIALISTS: This independent study package meets the criteria for a formally approved American Nurses Credentialing Center (ANCC) Activity . PESI, LLC is an approved provider by the American Psychological Association, which is recognized by the ANCC for behavioral health related activities.

Nurses completing these learner-directed materials will earn 2.0 contact hours.

Procedures:

1. Review the workbook that contains the written materials.

2. Review and study the recording.

3. If seeking credit, the following must be completed on the post-test/evaluation form:

> -Complete post test/evaluation in entirety; including your email address to receive your certificate much faster versus by mail.
> -Upon completion, mail to the address listed on the form, or fax to 1-800-554-9775, "Attention: CE Dept".

Your completed post test/evaluation will be graded. If you receive a passing score (70% and above), you will be emailed/faxed/mailed a certificate of successful completion with earned continuing education credits. (Please write your email address on the post test/evaluation form for fastest response.) If you do not pass the post-test, you will be sent a letter indicating areas of deficiency, and another post test to complete. The post-test must be resubmitted and receive a passing grade before credit can be awarded. We will allow you to re-take as many times as necessary to receive a certificate.

If you have any questions, please feel free to contact our customer service department at 1.800.844.8260.

Course Content

The workbook is a supplement to the Evidence-Based Treatment Planning for Depression DVD, which is focused on informing mental health therapists, addiction counselors, and students in these fields about empirically informed psychological treatment planning. The content in the DVD and workbook will examine the following: DSM criteria for depression, six steps in building a treatment plan, brief history of the empirically supported treatments movement, identified treatments for depression, treatment planning, and considerations for relapse prevention.

PESI LLC
PO BOX 1000
Eau Claire, WI 54702-1000

Evidence-Based Treatment Planning for Depression

PO BOX 1000
Eau Claire, WI 54702
800-844-8260

Any persons interested in receiving credit may photocopy this form, complete and return with a payment of $15.00 per person CE fee. A certificate of successful completion will be sent to you. To receive your certificate sooner than two weeks, rush processing is available for a fee of $10. Please attach check or include credit card information below.

Mail to: PESI, PO Box 1000, Eau Claire, WI 54702 or fax to PESI (800) 554-9775 (both sides)

CE Fee: $15: (Rush processing fee: $10)   **Total to be charged** _____

Credit Card #: _____ **Exp Date:** _____ **V-Code*:** _____
(*MC/VISA/Discover: last 3-digit # on signature panel on back of card.) (*American Express: 4-digit # above account # on face of card.)

	LAST	FIRST	M.I.

Name (please print): _____ _____ _____

Address: _____ Daytime Phone: _____

City: _____ State: _____ Zip Code: _____

Signature: _____ Email: _____

Date Completed: _____ Actual time (# of hours) taken to complete this offering: _____hours

Program Objectives After completing this publication, I have been able to achieve these objectives:

Explain the process and criteria for diagnosing depression	Yes	No
List the six steps in building a clear psychotherapy treatment plan	Yes	No
Examine how empirically supported treatments for depression have been identified	Yes	No
Examine the objectives and treatment interventions consistent with those of identified empirically supported treatments for depression	Yes	No
Explain how to construct a psychotherapy treatment plan and inform it with objectives and treatment interventions consistent with those identified empirically supported treatments for depression	Yes	No
Identify common considerations in the prevention of relapse of depression, as well as empirically supported relapse prevention interventions for depression	Yes	No

PESI LLC
PO BOX 1000
Eau Claire, WI 54702-1000

ZNT042140

CE Release Date: 3/31/10

Participant Profile:

1. Job Title: _____ Employment setting: _____

1. Which of the following best describes the process used in diagnosing depression?
a. Current (present) symptoms are assessed and compared to the criteria for the mood disorder.
b. Past and present mood episodes are assessed and then used to make the diagnosis of the mood disorder.
c. Past and present mood disorders are assessed and then used to make the diagnosis of the mood episode.
d. The level of clinical distress and disability is assessed and used to make the diagnosis of the mood disorder.

2. Which of the following symptoms MUST be present in the clinical picture to meet criteria for a major depressive episode?
a. Difficulty concentrating or a sleep disturbance.
b. Sadness or diminished interest.
c. Sadness or guilt.
d. Sadness or a sleep disturbance.

3. In a treatment plan, which of the following represents the incremental actions the client will take to reach his or her therapeutic goals?
a. Behavioral definitions.
b. Primary and secondary problem.
c. Short-term objectives.
d. Therapeutic interventions.

4. Which statement best describes the relationship between empirically supported treatment (ESTs) and an evidence-based practice (EBP)?
a. ESTs and an EBP are two acronyms for the same concept.
b. ESTs describe a more comprehensive treatment approach than an EBP.
c. Practitioners may use ESTs as part of providing an overall EBP.
d. Practitioners may use EBPs as part of providing an overall EST.

5. There are two ESTs for depression that have well-established efficacy for the treatment of depression according to the criteria used by APA's Division 12 to identify ESTs.

TRUE   FALSE

6. Which EST for depression places emphasis on increasing the client's involvement in activities that are likely to result in the client experiencing pleasure, a sense of mastery, or other emotionally rewarding consequences?
a. Behavioral Activation.
b. Cognitive Restructuring.
c. Interpersonal Therapy.
d. Problem-solving Therapy.

7. Which EST for depression has emphasized the assessment and treatment of grief and loss themes as a major focus of the therapy?
a. Behavioral Activation.
b. Cognitive Restructuring.
c. Interpersonal Therapy.
d. Problem-solving Therapy.

8. Which of the following examples is most consistent with the approach to empirically informing a treatment plan for depression recommended in this program?
a. The therapist incorporates into therapy assertiveness skills training.
b. The therapist incorporates into therapy the practice of asking the client to monitor their depressive feelings.
c. The therapist incorporates into therapy the objectives and interventions consistent with Problem-solving Therapy.
d. The therapist incorporates the use of an objective measure of depression to track treatment progress.

9. According to this program, an intervention used in relapse prevention for depression involves reviewing the application of skills learned in therapy to high-risk situations.

TRUE   FALSE

10. For depression, there is currently no empirical support for interventions focused on the prevention of relapse.

TRUE   FALSE

PESI LLC
PO BOX 1000
Eau Claire, WI 54702-1000